THE LOGIC OF CONDITIONALS

SYNTHESE LIBRARY

VOLUME 86

ERNEST W. ADAMS

THE LOGIC
OF CONDITIONALS

An Application of Probability to Deductive Logic

D. REIDEL PUBLISHING COMPANY

DORDRECHT-HOLLAND / BOSTON-U.S.A.

Library of Congress Cataloging in Publication Data

Adams, Ernest Wilcox, 1926–

    The Logic of conditionals.

    (Synthese library ; v. 86)
    Bibliography: p.
    Includes indexes.
    1. Conditionals (Logic) 2. Probabilities.
3. Counterfactuals (Logic) I. Title.
BC199.C56A3   160   75–20306
ISBN 90–277–0631–X

Published by D. Reidel Publishing Company,
P.O. Box 17, Dordrecht, Holland

Sold and distributed in the U.S.A., Canada, and Mexico
by D. Reidel Publishing Company, Inc.
306 Dartmouth Street, Boston,
Mass. 02116, U.S.A.
All Rights Reserved

Printed in The Netherlands by D. Reidel, Dordrecht

To Anne, Jimmy, and Billy

TABLE OF CONTENTS

PREFACE

Of the four chapters in this book, the first two discuss (albeit in considerably modified form) matters previously discussed in my papers 'On the Logic of Conditionals' [1] and 'Probability and the Logic of Conditionals' [2], while the last two present essentially new material. Chapter I is relatively informal and roughly parallels the first of the above papers in discussing the basic ideas of a probabilistic approach to the logic of the indicative conditional, according to which these constructions do not have truth values, but they do have probabilities (equal to conditional probabilities), and the appropriate criterion of soundness for inferences involving them is that it should not be possible for all premises of the inference to be probable while the conclusion is improbable. Applying this criterion is shown to have radically different consequences from the orthodox 'material conditional' theory, not only in application to the standard 'fallacies' of the material conditional, but to many forms (e.g., Contraposition) which have hitherto been regarded as above suspicion. Many more applications are considered in Chapter I, as well as certain related theoretical matters. The chief of these, which is the most important new topic treated in Chapter I (i.e., this topic has not been treated in my own earlier articles), is a discussion of the fundamentally important *triviality results* of David Lewis ([40], as yet, alas, unpublished, in spite of the fact that these results must be central to any probabilistic approach to logic). What these results imply is that if the assumptions of the probabilistic theory are right, then *no* purely truth-conditional 'logic' of the conditional can avoid difficulties of the sort arising in the fallacies of material implication, and an adequate theory of the conditional *must* consider other 'dimensions of rightness' besides truth, and other criteria of soundness besides the classical one that the truth of premises should be inconsistent with the falsity of conclusions.

Chapter II, which is the only chapter of the book involving original mathematics, parallels my earlier paper 'Probability and the Logic of Conditionals' in proving a number of general theorems concerning the properties of the probabilistic soundness criterion – that it should be impossible for the premises of an inference to be probable while its conclusion is improbable, the failure to satisfy which is what is wrong in the fallacies of material implication. The only thing to note about the present formulation is that the proofs have been radically simplified, essentially following the lines of related arguments given in my paper 'The Logic of "Almost All"' [4].

Chapter III is an attempt to argue for the rightness of the basic assumptions of the probabilistic theory (which entail the triviality results in turn), and to argue for the mistakenness of the assumptions of orthodox logic as it applies to conditionals. This argument involves what I regard as the most important new ideas in the present book, though these are probably the ones which will be least sympathetically received either by orthodox logicians or by the new breed of 'philosophical logicians'. What I try to show is that probabilistic theory meets but orthodox theory fails to meet a *pragmatic requirement of adequacy* for theories of truth and soundness: namely, that it should be possible to demonstrate that persons are best advised to try to arrive at conclusions which are 'true' according to the tenets of the theory, and are best off reasoning in accord with principles which the theory holds to be sound. Without going into detail, an example from Section III.5 illustrates the failure of orthodox logic's assumed *material truth* definition (giving the truth conditions for conditionals) to meet this requirement. Imagine a man about to eat some very good and non-poisonous mushrooms who is informed "if you eat those mushrooms you will be poisoned", which leads the man not to eat the mushrooms, while making the statement 'true' (i.e., materially true) at the same time. Obviously the man would have been better off *not* to have arrived at this allegedly 'true' conclusion, and this type of example should make it questionable that reasoners should *want* to be guided in their reasoning by the principles of orthodox logic, if those are designed to lead them to conclusions which are 'true' in this unwanted sense. The positive argument of Chapter III is to show (at least in limited circumstances) that the proposed probabilistic theory does satisfy the pragmatic requirement, the demonstration of which requires us to consider systematically how people *act* on conclusions of conditional form which they might arrive at, and how the wanted or unwanted results of these actions are related to the 'rightness' of the conclusions acted on. I should perhaps acknowledge immediately that the adequacy argument is anything but definitive, and perhaps the strongest claim that can be made for the significance of these arguments is that these are the sorts of considerations which *ought* to be taken into account in evaluating any proposed logical theory whose basic assumptions are questionable.

Chapter IV concerns counterfactuals, and covers much the same ground as another article 'Prior Probabilities and Counterfactual Conditionals' [5] which I had originally expected to appear prior to the book, but which will now be rendered obsolete by the book because of important modifications of the theory. The core of both the article and the book is an *epistemic past tense* hypothesis concerning the analysis of the counterfactual, according to which the probability of a counterfactual conditional at the time of its utterance equals a *prior probability* of the corresponding indicative conditional (i.e., its probability upon some prior occasion). This is argued to explain a variety of logical phenomena involving the counterfactual (possibly the most interesting of which is its use in 'explanation' contexts, where it clearly does *not* imply the falsity of its antecedent), and to yield a deeper understanding of inference 'processes' like a typical kind of *Modus Tollens*, in which 'inferring a conclusion' is reconceptualized as a phenomenon of *probability change* resulting from new premise acquisition. The chief difference between the present chapter and the article is that I no longer maintain that the epistemic past tense interpretation can be stretched to cover all uses of the counterfactual, and there are significant uses, especially related to *dispositional* concepts, which do not conform to the analysis. In consequence, I would now argue only that something like the epistemic past interpretation should play an important *part* in an adequate general analysis of the counterfactual, but lacking such an analysis it may be useful to consider the implications of the limited hypothesis.

A word should be said about the mathematical background presupposed of readers of this book. I should like to think that the proposed theory would be of interest to logicians generally, and I have accordingly kept mathematical technicalities to a minimum consistent with a reasonable demand for brevity. As noted, the only original and even slightly difficult mathematics is confined to Chapter II, and nearly all parts of the other chapters can be read independently. Elementary probability formulas are occasionally employed, which should be intelligible to persons with only a small acquaintance with the formalism of probability, and occasionally some slight mathematical argument, which will be obvious to anyone knowing something of probability theory, is needed to justify these formulas, but which is omitted in order to avoid obscuring the fundamental issues at stake. Above all I have tried to avoid the appearance of mathematical display for its own sake, since I am most anxious that this work not be dismissed as just another of the puerile mathematical exercises in logical 'system building' which have become only too common in recent years (realistically, I must suppose that the book will be dismissed in this way by many).

It is impossible to acknowledge my indebtedness individually to all of the many students and colleagues whose ideas and criticisms have helped to shape my own ideas on conditionals, but I am particularly grateful to Professors Brian Skyrms, William Cooper, and David Shwayder. Skyrms has most influenced my thinking about counterfactuals, has gone much further than I have in investigating relations between counterfactuals and *laws*, and a book which he is now engaged in writing on that subject will very much deepen the rather sketchy ideas presented here. Cooper's work has been most helpful to me in its systematic analysis of all sorts of uses of indicative conditionals in ordinary speech and writing, and again a forthcoming book [12] will go much further than I have in describing the ordinary language 'data' which any theory of the conditional must account for. Shwayder is the person who first suggested to me that I try to draw my ideas concerning conditionals together and present them in book form, and his influence here is most evident in the earlier sections of Chapter III, concerning the relation between belief and action. He also very kindly provided me with detailed criticisms and comments on those sections, which show that some aspects of the theory presented there require serious modification. Unfortunately, pressure to meet a publishing deadline has prevented me from taking these criticisms into account here, and all I can say here is that I intend to more fittingly acknowledge them in later work in the way that matters most: namely by demonstrating their influence on my own views.

I should like also to express my thanks to Savannah Ross, Yulia Motofuji, Julie Martinson, and Katy Dreith who have wrestled with the manuscript of this book in various stages of its preparation, and especially to Ruth Suzuki whose excellent and rapid typing alone allowed the manuscript to be completed in a last mad scramble to finish in time to meet the publisher's deadline. Finally, a grateful salutation is in order to the persons to whom this book is dedicated, my wife Anne, and sons Jimmy and Billy, who have lived with and borne with the writing of this book almost as much as I have, and who I hope most of all will be pleased with the result.

CHAPTER I

THE INDICATIVE CONDITIONAL

1. A PROBABILISTIC CRITERION OF SOUNDNESS FOR DEDUCTIVE INFERENCES

Our objective in this section is to establish a *prima facie* case for the appropriateness of assessing the soundness or rationality of deductive inferences in terms of a new requirement or criterion of rationality beyond the usual truth-conditional criterion: that it should be impossible for the premises of an inference to be true while its conclusion is false. The proposed supplementary criterion results when the words 'probable' and 'improbable' are substituted for 'true' and 'false', respectively, in the truth-conditional criterion, yielding the *probabilistic soundness criterion*: it should be impossible for the premises of an inference to be probable while its conclusion is improbable. This formulation is vague and we shall want to clarify it later, but our present concern is with the legitimacy of demanding that deductive inferences satisfy something like this requirement if they are to be regarded as 'rational'.

Observe that where the premises or grounds of a deductive inference are not themselves absolute certainties – by far the most common case outside of mathematics – the conclusion of the inference will not be an absolute certainty if it depends on the premises. Example: you initially believe "either A or B will teach the class", then learn that A will not teach the class, and thereupon 'deduce' that B will teach it.[1] In the nature of things the premises are not the sorts of propositions concerning which absolute certainty is possible (at least at the time the reasoning is represented as taking place), and it is obvious that the conclusion could not be a certainty either in such circumstances.

Hypothesis: in a situation where a reasoner must reason from somewhat uncertain or fallible premises, he should want to reason in accord with principles which lead from probable premises to probable conclusions – because he wants to arrive at probable conclusions. Given such a reasoner's interests, it will be appropriate for him to apply the probabilistic soundness 'test' to reasoning patterns and processes to help him to determine whether they will guide him to the kinds of conclusions he hopes to reach.

Is there a difference in practice between truth-conditional soundness (soundness according to the truth-conditional criterion) and probabilistic soundness (soundness according to the as yet vague probabilistic criterion)? Given an intuitively very plausible assumption about the relation between truth and probability, it would seem that the answer to the foregoing question should be: *very little*. Roughly stated, the assumption is that *the probability of a proposition is the same as the probability that it is true*. A more exact statement is that the probability of a proposition is the sum of the probabilities of the possible states of affairs in which the proposition would be true (more generally, the *measure* the set of these possible states of affairs). The consequence of this assumption is: *if an inference is truth-conditionally sound then the uncertainty of its conclusion cannot exceed the sum of the uncertainties of its premises* (where *uncertainty* is here defined as probability of falsity – not to be confused with the entropic uncertainty measure of Information Theory).[2]

It is hard to overemphasize the importance of the foregoing as a justification for working exclusively with truth-conditional soundness in the analysis of inferences involving propositions to which the "probability equals probability of truth" assumption applies. The theorem tells us that if there are only a few premises, each with a 'reasonably small' uncertainty (and what 'reasonably small' is will vary with circumstances), a truth-conditionally implied conclusion cannot be very improbable – though it can obviously be more improbable than any individual premise. It is only where there are many premises whose uncertainties can 'acumulate' in an unfortunate way (as in the Lottery Paradox – see [39]), that we find serious divergence between the truth-conditional and probabilistic criterion, and truth-conditional soundness becomes a necessary but not a sufficient condition for probabilistic soundness. In such cases common sense supports the appropriateness of insisting on probabilistic soundness, since it is patent that even truth-conditionally sound inferences from a lot of 'shaky data' can be highly unreliable.

So we know that we must watch out for uncertainty accumulation in deductive inferences from too many premises. However, this sort of divergence between truth-conditional and probabilistic soundness will not concern us in what follows – although there are many interesting methodological and mathematical problems connected with the analysis of this phenomenon, some of which are discussed in a joint paper by Howard Levine and the author [7]. What we want to argue next is that there is a much more radical divergence between the two soundness criteria in application to inferences involving conditional propositions, which is ultimately traceable to the failure of the probability equals probability of truth assumption in application to conditionals.

2. CONDITIONALS AND CONDITIONAL PROBABILITIES

The fundamental assumption of this work is: *the probability of an indicative conditional of the form "if A is the case then B is" is a conditional probability*. This assumption, which has been suggested and then apparently abandoned by such authors as Ramsey [45] and Jeffrey [33][3], is that the probability of "if *A* then *B*" should equal the *ratio* of the probability of "*A* and *B*" to the probability of *A* (ratio of conjunction of antecedent and consequent to antecedent). For the present we shall have to let the assumption rest on its immediate intuitive plausibility (or the plausibility which we hope to give it by considering some of its applications), but it must be acknowledged that the assumption is quite controversial at the present juncture – largely, one suspects, because its implications are radical.[4] Chapter III of this book will attempt a justification of the assumption by appeal to 'appropriateness' considerations – what one *wants* of conclusions he arrives at of conditional form. For now we will confine ourselves to considering applications.

First note that the ratio or conditional probability measure of the probability of "if *A* then *B*" differs from the probability of the corresponding material conditional. Symbolizing, let the material conditional with antecedent *A* and consequent *B* be written $A \supset B$, and let the corresponding 'ordinary English indicative conditional' be abbreviated $A \Rightarrow B$. Writing probabilities with the function symbol '*p*' and uncertainties with '*u*' (where uncertainty equals 1 minus probability), we have important the formula:

$$(1) \qquad u(A \Rightarrow B) = \frac{u(A \supset B)}{p(A)}.$$

Illustration: Let A be "a number less than three will be rolled" (concerning the roll of a fair die) and let B be "an even number will be rolled." The conditional probability of B given A, which we are postulating is equal to $p(A \Rightarrow B)$, is equal to $p(A \,\&\, B)$ divided by $p(A)$, which is easily seen to be 1/6 divided by 2/6. It follows that $p(A \Rightarrow B)$ should be 1/2, and so $u(A \Rightarrow B)$ should be $1 - 1/2 = 1/2$. On the other hand there are five ways in six in which the material conditional $A \supset B$ can be true, hence $p(A \supset B)$ $= 5/6$ and $u(A \supset B) = 1/6$. Dividing $u(A \supset B)$ by $p(A) = 2/6$ gives $u(A \Rightarrow B)$, as stipulated by Equation (1). What the equation shows in general is that *the uncertainty of the indicative conditional is never less than that of the corresponding material conditional, and is in fact greater except in the cases where: (1) both uncertainties are 0, or (2) their common antecedent, A, has probability 1.*

The discrepancy between the material conditional's probability and that of the corresponding indicative conditional explains why it would be irrational to make inferences in accord with one of the notorious 'fallacies' of material implication, not because such an inference would fail to meet the truth-conditional test for soundness, but because it would fail to meet the probabilistic one. The fallacious pattern is to infer "if A then B" from "not A", which can be written symbolically with the premise above and the conclusion below a line:

$$\frac{- A}{A \Rightarrow B}.$$

The inference of the material conditional $A \supset B$ from $-A$ is truth-conditionally sound so it follows that the uncertainty of $A \supset B$ can be no greater than that of $-A$: $u(A \supset B) \leqslant u(-A)$. However, the indicative conditional's uncertainty, $u(A \Rightarrow B)$, which is what we are interested in, will generally be greater than $u(A \supset B)$, and in fact will ordinarily be much greater in this case since $u(A \Rightarrow B)$ equals $u(A \supset B)/p(A)$, and $p(A)$ will be small because $p(-A)$ is close to 1. We will see shortly that in fact the premise probability $p(-A)$ can be 'arbitrarily close to certainty' while the conclusion probability, $p(A \Rightarrow B)$, can equal 0, and this must surely be the reason why persons do not in practice normally reason in accord with this fallacious pattern.

Does the fault in the usual logical analysis of inferences involving conditionals lie solely in the 'mistaken' ascription of the material conditional's truth-conditions to the indicative conditional? We want to argue next, adapting to our purpose a most important *triviality result* of David Lewis [40], that the problem is much deeper. *If the conditional probability measure for conditional's probabilities is correct, and given other standard assumptions of probability theory, there is no way of attaching dichotomous truth values to conditionals in such a way that their probabilities will equal their probabilities of being true.* The foregoing would imply that it is hopeless to hunt for the 'right' truth-conditions for conditionals which can be used in testing the truth-conditional soundness of inferences involving such propositions, if it is also required that truth-conditional soundness should closely approximate probabilistic soundness in the way it does in the case of inferences involving only 'factual' propositions. This may be connected with our reluctance to apply the term 'true' in the standard logical way to conditionals (we will have more to say about this in Chapter III), but whatever the fate of the truth-conditional analysis of the conditional, we can at least say that the foregoing implies that truth-conditional soundness cannot be the unique and central criterion of rationality for inferences involving conditionals that it is for inferences involving only factual propositions. Again, it would be hard to overstress the importance of this conclusion, for it would mark an unmistakable limit to the reach of truth-conditionality.

Now the argument. The more definitive argument is somewhat technical, and it may help to preface it with a simpler one which is not entirely conclusive. Note that the conditional probability $p(A \Rightarrow B)$ is *almost* a function of the probabilities $p(A)$ and $p(A \& B)$. The only exceptional case is that in which $p(A) = p(A \& B) = 0$ and the ratio of the two probabilities is undefined.[5] Ignoring this difficulty and supposing for the moment that $p(A \Rightarrow B)$ is *always* a function of $p(A \& B)$ and $p(A)$, it would follow that the truth-value, $t(A \Rightarrow B)$, of $A \Rightarrow B$ should be a function of the truth-values $t(A \& B)$ and $t(A)$. For, if the latter were not so there would exist propositions A_1 and B_1 and A_2 and B_2, and a possible assignment of truth-values given by a function t (t's values would be truth-values in some 'possible state of affairs') such that $t(A_1) = t(A_2)$ and $t(A_1 \& B_1) = t(A_2 \& B_2)$, but $t(A_1 \Rightarrow B_1) \neq t(A_2 \Rightarrow B_2)$. If the foregoing were really possible, then it should also be possible for these facts to become known as certainties: i.e., propositions known to be true should have probability 1 while those known to be false should have probability

0. It would follow from this, though, that $p(A_1) = p(A_2)$ and $p(A_1 \& B_1) = p(A_2 \& B_2)$ while $p(A_1 \Rightarrow B_1) \neq p(A_2 \Rightarrow B_2)$, contradicting the probability functionality assumption.[6]

In order to get round the difficulty caused by the fact that $p(A \Rightarrow B)$ is not defined when $p(A)$ is 0, we proceed as follows. To simplify, let truth-functions, t, have the values 1 and 0 (1 for truth and 0 for falsehood), from which it follows directly that truth-functions satisfy the formal laws (the Kolmogorov axioms [36]) for unconditional probability functions. Assuming that conditionals have truth-values, however, it would also follow that $t(A \Rightarrow B)$ was always defined and had the value 1 or 0, no matter what the truth or probability of A and $A \& B$ might be. Now we make two essential assumptions whose significance will be discussed below: that any truth function is a possible probability function and any 50-50 'mixture' of truth-functions is a possible probability function. Intuitively, what this amounts to is assuming that for any possible state of affairs it is possible that it be certain to be the actual state of affairs, and for any two possible states of affairs it is possible that each have probability .5 of being the actual state of affairs. The latter implies that if t_1 and t_2 are two truth-functions, then the 50-50 mixture $1/2 t_1 + 1/2 t_2$ should satisfy the laws of probability, and furthermore this should be the case even in application to conditionals.

Now make use of the fact that for any probability function, p, it follows from the law of conditional probability that so long as p is defined

$$p(A) \cdot p(A \Rightarrow B) = p(A \& B).$$

The above should hold in particular for truth-functions, t, and 50-50 mixtures $1/2 t_1 + 1/2 t_2$, hence it would follow that

$$t(A) \cdot t(A \Rightarrow B) = t(A \& B) = t(A) \cdot t(B)$$

(the second equation simply being the rule relating the truth-value of a conjunction to the truth-values of the conjuncts). Also it follows by simple algebra that:

$$(t_1(A) - t_2(A)) \cdot (t_1(A \Rightarrow B) - t_2(A \Rightarrow B)) = 0.$$

The above two equations imply that if there is *any* possible state of affairs, t, such that $t(A) = 0$ (A is not logically true), then for any B, B must have the same truth value in all states of affairs in which A is true. But this entails in turn that there could not exist *three* truth-functions, t_1, t_2, and t_3, which were 'distinguishable' in the sense that there existed propositions A, B, and C such that $t_1(A) \neq t_2(A)$, $t_1(B) \neq t_3(B)$, and $t_2(C) \neq t_3(C)$.

The upshot of the foregoing is that the assumption that conditionals are truth-functional *and* their probabilities are conditional probabilities leads to the conclusion that there can be only *two* possible states of affairs and associated truth-functions – which would further imply that there could be only four probability values. This 'trivializes' truth and probability.

Various attitudes which one may adopt towards the foregoing triviality result will be commented on in a moment, together with the connection between the present result and Lewis's own results. First, however, it should be noted that *if* all of the assumptions leading to the result are accepted, then the futility of a truth-conditional analysis of the conditional which is adequate as a basis for the theory of the rationality of inferences involving it is established. This implies equally to the familiar material conditional analysis and to more recently proposed 'possible worlds' theories such as that of Stalnaker [53]. Truth conditions are just not enough.

Now to the assumptions, possible attitudes towards them, and their connections with Lewis's assumptions and results. Fundamentally, and somewhat roughly, there were four basic assumptions: (1) probabilities satisfy the usual laws of unconditional probability (Kolmogorov axioms), (2) probabilities of conditionals, where defined, are conditional probabilities, (3) truth-values, including those of conditionals, are always defined, and (4) truth functions and probability mixtures of truth functions are probability functions. It is possible to avoid the triviality results by giving up or modifying any one of the four assumptions. Lewis himself gives up (2) – that probabilities of conditionals are conditional probabilities. Van Fraassen [60] in effect gives up (4) and shows that the other three assumptions are consistent and don't entail triviality. Skyrms [50] has proposed modifying (1), but only in application to conditional propositions and compounds containing them as constituents. The author's opinion, of course, is that either (3) must be given up, or it must be admitted that probability does not equal probability of truth (which is implicit in (4)). Which of these attitudes is 'right' is clearly something which cannot be decided on formal grounds alone, and we will argue in Chapter III, where the matter is examined, that something more than 'intuitive appeal' must enter in. For the moment we must let the matter rest, with the understanding that it will be taken up in Chapter III, and that in the meantime we are exploring the consequences of only one 'way out' of the triviality results.

Finally, we should note the connection between the present result and Lewis's one, and the assumptions on which it was based. What Lewis showed explicitly was that probabilities couldn't attach to compounds containing conditional constituents and still satisfy all of a number of desirable laws. It is obvious that this result must be closely connected to the possibility of attaching truth-values to conditionals in such a way that probability equals probability of truth – for if the latter were possible there should be no difficulty about attaching probabilities to truth-functional compounds of conditionals. This matter will be returned to in Section 8.

Lewis's basic assumptions differ from the four made here in that in place of our assumption (4) (that truth-functions and probability mixtures of them are probability functions) Lewis assumes that *probabilities change by conditionalization* (the probability attaching to B after A is learned to be the case should equal that previously attaching to $A \Rightarrow B$). Both our assumption and Lewis's have the effect of assuring the existence of a *space* of possible probability functions which has a 'structure' in that these functions are interrelated in certain ways. Both of these structural assumptions (i.e., assumptions about the structure of the probability function space) are commonly made and they are closely connected. Probability change by conditionalization is probably the more fundamental 'probability transformation operation', but probability mixing is a kind of *inverse* of this. Where conditionalizing never increases and generally decreases entropy (information-theoretic uncertainty), mixing generally increases it. More importantly, the 'pure probabilities' (in our case truth-functions) which are involved in a mixture (e.g. a 50-50 mixture of truth-functions) can generally be recovered from the mixture by conditionalization, and this holds of all of the mixtures considered in our argument. In any event, it becomes clear that probability space structure assumptions, which have until recently received scant attention in the literature on the foundations of probability (Teller [57] is an important exception to this), require careful examination if triviality results and their implications for the logic of conditionals are to be evaluated.

3. Informal Assessment of Some Patterns of Conditional Inference

The objective of this section is to introduce an informal but pedagogically useful method for assessing inference schemata involving conditionals, and illustrate its usefulness in application to certain well known patterns. The method involves the use of something like the Venn diagram for representing probabilities visually, which has the advantage of avoiding explicit work with numerical probabilities.

We begin by supposing that all possible states of affairs are represented by points within a suitably chosen rectangle, and that factual propositions like A and B are represented by the subregions of the rectangle containing those possible states of affairs in which the propositions are true, as illustrated in Figure 1 below:

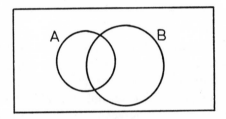

Fig. 1.

So far we have no more than a Venn diagram, which has the advantage of pictorially representing not only the regions corresponding to atomic propositions A and B, but of representing all of their truth-functional combinations like $-A$ and A & B at the same time.[7] Conditional propositions like $A \Rightarrow B$ are *not* assumed to correspond to subregions of the rectangle – the diagrammatic expression of the fact that conditionals are not assumed to be true or false in possible states of affairs.

Probabilities are now introduced into the picture by identifying the *areas* of the subregions corresponding to particular factual formulas with the probabilities of the formulas – with the stipulation that the area of the entire rectangle is assumed to equal 1. In effect, the probability of a formula is represented as the probability that a point picked at random within the rectangle should lie within the corresponding region. Again we get a representation of the probabilities of truth-conditional compounds as a bonus along with the probabilities of their atomic constituents, and in effect the diagram gives a visual expression of the standard laws of unconditional probability (e.g., $p(-A) = 1 - p(A)$). There is also a sense in which the diagram represents a *possible probabilistic state of affairs*, where propositions corresponding to large regions are represented as probable while those corresponding to small regions are represented as improbable. Note that each possible probabilistic state of affairs 'comprehends' *all* possible truth-conditional states of affairs.

Finally, the probability of the conditional $A \Rightarrow B$ is identified in the diagram with the *proportion* of subregion A which lies inside subregion B. If most of region A lies inside region B, this is interpreted to mean that the probability of $A \Rightarrow B$ is high, and if most of A lies outside of B the probability of the conditional is low. Given the conventions already adopted, the probability of $A \Rightarrow B$ is represented as the ratio of the probability of A & B to the probability of A – the conditional probability. Note that whereas unconditional propositions correspond to regions inside the rectangle and their probabilities are represented by the areas of these regions, conditionals are not represented in this way and their probabilities are not represented by areas. This is the diagrammatic expression of the fact that conditionals' probabilities are not probabilities of truth.

Before putting our probabilistic Venn diagrams to work, two essential limitations should be noted. One is that if $p(A) = 0$ then the probability of $A \Rightarrow B$ is not defined, since in this case the proportion corresponding is not defined. Just how serious a limitation this is is difficult to say, and throughout what follows we shall just ignore the 'zero antecedent probability case', with the understanding that when it is taken into account it may alter our picture of conditionals and their probabilities, and their logical interrelations.[8] The second limitation is that while we have represented the probabilities of atomic factual propositions *and* their truth-functional combinations, we have not represented the probabilities of truth-functional combinations of conditionals like conjunctions, disjunctions and denials of them. This exclusion of truth-functional compounds of conditionals is of course the diagrammatic expression of the fact that there are fundamental difficulties connected with attaching probabilities to such constructions, which will be returned to in Section I.8. The thing to keep in mind for now is that our probabilistically interpreted Venn diagrams represent factual and *simple* conditional propositions – conditionals with factual antecedents and consequents – but not more complicated constructions.

The use to which Venn diagrams are to be put is in depicting *probabilistic counterexamples* to inference schemata, in which the premises of a schema are represented as probable while its conclusion is represented as improbable. Once this is done we seek concrete examples of propositions whose probabilities fit the conditions represented by the 'diagrammatic counterexample'. To illustrate, consider the two familiar 'fallacious' patterns of material implication:

$$\frac{-A}{A \Rightarrow B} \qquad \frac{B}{A \Rightarrow B}$$

(to infer $A \Rightarrow B$ either from $-A$ or from B). Figure 2 below represents simultaneously a probabilistic counterexample to both schemata:

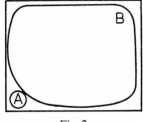

Fig. 2.

In the figure $A \Rightarrow B$ is represented as having probability 0 since none of region A lies inside of B, while both $-A$ and B are represented as probable since both of the corresponding regions nearly fill the rectangle. Hence we have a possible probabilistic state of affairs in which both $-A$ and B are probable while $A \Rightarrow B$ is improbable, and this shows the two schemata to be probabilistically unsound (they fail the probabilistic soundness test). The analysis is completed by finding real propositions A and B whose probabilities fit the required conditions. These are: (1) A must be highly improbable, (2) B must be very probable, and (3) A must 'probabilistically exclude' B. Examples:

A = it will not rain in Berkeley next year
B = it will rain in Berkeley next year.

The reader may decide for himself whether he would accept and assert $-A$ or B, and whether he would deduce $A \Rightarrow B$ therefrom.

Some observations are in order before proceeding to other inference patterns. First, it must be reiterated that our probabilistic counter-examples do *not* show that the inference schemata to which they apply are truth-conditionally unsound: they show rather that the schemata fail to satisfy *another* requirement of rationality which it is also desirable that inferences satisfy. Second, the reason why persons reasoning in real life should want their inferences to satisfy the probabilistic requirement has something to do with the fact that ordinarily they cannot be absolutely certain of the premises from which they reason. This is represented pictorially in Figure 2, by the fact that it was essential in drawing that figure that the premises $-A$ and B *not* be represented as complete certainties. Intuitively, it is plausible that truth-conditional soundness is enough, so long as premise uncertainties can be neglected. Of course this ignores the fact that in application to factual inferences truth-conditional soundness is 'almost' the same as probabilistic soundness, whereas the two concepts differ much more radically in application to inferences involving conditionals. This suggests that the conditional has a special connection to uncertainty, and the second fallacy of material implication (to infer $A \Rightarrow B$ from B) brings this out. One common use of conditionals is to express hedges to factual assertions which are not perfectly certain. Thus one may say "the performance will be held outdoors; *but* if it rains it will be held indoors." Obviously not any hedge $A \Rightarrow B$ on a factual assertion B (or $-B$) is rational, and this is why the fallacy of the inference of $A \Rightarrow B$ from B is obvious, since it suggests that one may never hedge a factual assertion.

Two technical comments may also be made. Note that while it was essential for the premises $-A$ and B in the above examples to be less than complete certainties, they could obviously have been 'as probable as desired' short of certainty. This generalizes to arbitrary inference schemata which are truth-conditionally sound (in the sense that they would be sound if the conditionals involved were material conditionals) but not probabilistically sound; it is always possible to find possible probabilistic states of affairs in which their premises are as probable as desired short of certainty while their conclusions are as improbable as desired short of certain falsity. This is shown in Theorem 3.2 of Chapter II.

Second, the concrete counterinstance to both of the fallacious schemata was of the form

$$\frac{-A}{A \Rightarrow -A}$$

whose conclusion has the form of a *probabilistic self-contradiction*, $A \Rightarrow -A$. Such a proposition necessarily has probability 0 (except possibly in the troublesome case in which A has probability 0). This suggests the appropriateness of formulating probabilistic inconsistency criteria which are to truth-conditional inconsistency as probabilistic soundness is to truth-conditional soundness. This possibility is explored in Section I.9, and is further developed in Chapter II, where probabilistic consistency provides the basis for a simple approach to the mathematical theory of probabilistic soundness.

Turning to other schemata, we would not expect schemata which are truth-conditionally unsound like the conditional inversion schema

$$\frac{A \Rightarrow B}{B \Rightarrow A}$$

to be probabilistically sound. Nonetheless such schemata are not without interest because they sometimes possess a certain plausibility which one might hope to explain on probabilistic grounds, and inversion in particular is interesting because it is closely related to the *confirmation* 'inference' in which persons initially accepting $A \Rightarrow B$ and then learning B are apt not to 'infer' A, but to regard A as more probable than before. Figure 3 confirms our expectation concerning the probabilistic unsoundness of inversion:

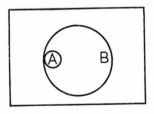

Fig. 3.

The figure also tells us what to look for in concrete counterinstances to the schema: (1) A should be improbable, (2) B should be considerably more probable than A, and (3) A should 'probabilistically imply' B in the sense that if A is the case then B is likely. Propositions fitting these requirements are:

$A =$ there will be a terrific cloudburst tomorrow
$B =$ it will rain tomorrow.

Once again the reader may consult his intuitions as to whether he would accept and affirm $A \Rightarrow B$, and whether he would infer $B \Rightarrow A$.

Three remarks on the inversion schema may be made. First, it illustrates our earlier rule that probabilistically unsound schemata can have arbitrarily certain premises short of perfect certainty while their conclusions are arbitrarily improbable. In the inversion case, though, the premise may be perfectly certain while the conclusion *almost* but not quite has probability 0. Second, the inversion case is an instance of the general rule that any truth-conditionally unsound schema with probabilistically consistent premises is also probabilistically unsound. Except where premises are probabilistically inconsistent, truth-conditional soundness is a necessary but usually not sufficient condition for probabilistic soundness. In a sense, then, probabilistic soundness is a stricter soundness requirement than truth-conditional soundness. Finally, Figure 3 gives some hint concerning the partial 'plausibility' of conditional inversion, which might explain its appeal to the logically unsophisticated. The figure suggests that where A and B do not stand in the special relation in which A is much less probable than B, conditional inversion may not be so irrational after all.

So far we have considered schemata which are truth-conditionally sound but intuitively irrational (the fallacies of material implication) and a schema which is truth-conditionally unsound (conditional inversion), but we have not considered any which are both truth-conditionally and intuitively rational. One such is a version of *contraposition*:

$$\frac{B \Rightarrow - A}{A \Rightarrow - B}.$$

Intuition and orthodox theory to the contrary however, Figure 3 also suggests the probabilistic unsoundness of contraposition, since it depicts almost all of B lying outside of A (hence $B \Rightarrow -A$ is probable) while all of A lies inside B (hence $A \Rightarrow -B$ has probability 0). Furthermore the propositions A and B giving a concrete counterinstance to inversion also provide a counterinstance to contraposition. One might well accept and affirm $B \Rightarrow -A$, "if it rains tomorrow there will not be a terrific cloudburst", but not infer $A \Rightarrow -B$, "if there is a terrific cloudburst tomorrow it will not rain." Of course, if one accepts the probabilistic unsoundness of contraposition he is in a dilemma: what is to be made of all of the real life reasoning which seems to be of this form? It is too much to condemn it as irrational *simpliciter*. We will argue in the next section that most such reasoning *is* rational, only, it is not rational *in virtue of being of the contraposition form*. Where such inferences are rational it is because further conditions are satisfied which usually obtain when persons are *told* propositions of the form $B \Rightarrow -A$, which are not part of the meaning of the proposition.

Similar observations apply to the even more important schema of inference of a conditional from a disjunction:

$$\frac{A \vee B}{-A \Rightarrow B}.$$

Reasoning after this fashion is ubiquitous in daily life, and the pattern is theoretically important because if it were sound it would justify treating the indicative conditional as a material conditional for logical purposes. Figure 4 shows however that the pattern is probabilistically unsound:

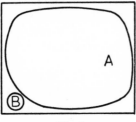

Fig. 4.

Concrete propositions fitting the requirements of Figure 4 are:

$A =$ it will rain in Berkeley next year
$B =$ it will snow in Berkeley next year.

One would assert $A \vee B$, "either it will rain or it will snow in Berkeley next year", but it would be paradoxical to infer $-A \Rightarrow B$, "if it doesn't rain then it will snow in Berkeley next year." Again, we are driven to inquire into the rationality of common real life instances of the pattern just brought into question. As with contraposition, we will argue in the next section that *most* such reasoning is rational, but not solely in virtue of being of instances of the pattern.

We conclude this section by noting the probabilistic unsoundness of three inference schemata of both practical and theoretical importance, each of which involves three atomic formulas. We begin with the *Hypothetical Syllogism* which is not only frequently employed (apparently), but which appears to be implicit in chains of reasoning from 'assumptions'. Figure 5 shows the pattern not to be probabilistically sound:

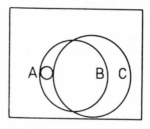

Fig. 5.

Examples of propositions whose probabilities fit the requirements depicted in Figure 5 would arise in a hypothetical situation in which Smith and Jones are the only candidates for a public office of which Smith is the incumbent, and Smith has announced his intention of retiring to private life in the event of his defeat. Let

A = Smith will die before the election
B = Jones will win the election
C = Smith will retire after the election.

Here it would be proper to affirm both "if Smith dies before the election Jones will win" and "if Jones wins then Smith will retire", but it would obviously be irrational to infer "if Smith dies before the election he will retire." Again we want to inquire further, rather than condemn all reasoning after the Hypothetical Syllogism pattern to total irrationality.

This matter will be discussed further in Section 5, where it will be argued that what we are accustomed to call Hypothetical Syllogism inference is really improperly represented in that form.

A pattern which is closely related to the Hypothetical Syllogism and which will be argued to have considerable theoretical importance is what we will baptize *Antecedent Restriction*:

$$\frac{B \Rightarrow C}{(A \ \& \ B) \Rightarrow C}.$$

Obviously Figure 5 also depicts a probabilistic counterexample to this inference, and the hypothetical examples above furnish a concrete counter-instance. One might affirm "If Jones wins the election then Smith will retire" but it would be absurd to infer "if Smith dies before the election and Jones wins then Smith will retire." It is interesting that the second fallacy of material implication

$$\frac{C}{A \Rightarrow C}$$

can be viewed as a special case of antecedent restriction, with B replaced by an arbitrary tautology. Counterinstances to the second fallacy become *ipso facto* counterinstances to the Antecedent Restriction inference schema.

An important partial inverse to Antecedent Restriction also appears to be quite common in everyday life:

$$\frac{(A \ \& \ B) \Rightarrow C, A}{B \Rightarrow C}.$$

This pattern is most easily seen to be probabilistically unsound by observing that it reduces essentially to the fallacious schema

$$\frac{A}{B \Rightarrow A}$$

in the special case in which C is set equal to A. Thus, we may set

$$A = C = \text{The performance will be outdoors}$$
$$B = \text{it will rain}.$$

We might affirm both "if the performance is held outdoors and it rains then the performance will be held outdoors" and "the performance will be held outdoors", but be unwilling to infer "if it rains the performance will be held outdoors." We will have more to say about this pattern in Section 5.

Having noted some particular logical phenomena involving the conditional, some of them perhaps unexpected, it is time to look deeper, and to seek some generalities. Two questions arise immediately: (1) Are there *any* conditional inference patterns for which probabilistic counter-examples *can't* be given? (2) What are we to say about real life reasoning (even mathematical reasoning) which appears to conform to probabilistically unsound patterns? The first of these questions will be the main concern of Chapter II, and in the remainder of this chapter we will be concerned with partial soundness and related matters.

4. PARTIAL SOUNDNESS AND CONVERSATIONAL IMPLICATURE CONSIDERATIONS RELATING TO CONTRAPOSITION AND INFERENCES OF CONDITIONALS FROM DISJUNCTIONS

We have suggested that the way to approach the question of the status of real life inferences which appear to be of probabilistically unsound forms is to consider the *special circumstances* in which such reasoning *is* rational, and to ask whether it is plausible that those circumstances prevail in situations where people reason after the questionable patterns. Vaguely, we may call the special circumstances in which an inference pattern is probabilistically sound its conditions of *partial rationality*. Contraposition and the inference of a conditional from a disjunction are not universally (probabilistically) sound, but they are plausibly sound in a wide variety of circumstances.

Restricting ourselves to inferences involving only factual and simple conditional propositions, two rules relating uncertainties of premises to conclusion uncertainties throw light on partial rationality conditions. These are: (1) The uncertainty of a *factual* conclusion of a truth-conditionally sound inference cannot exceed the sum of the uncertainties of the premises, whether or not the premises include conditionals. (2) The uncertainty of an indicative conditional equals the uncertainty of the corresponding material conditional divided by the probability of its antecedent (Equation (1)). Combining these we get: the uncertainty of a conditional conclusion of a truth-conditionally sound inference cannot exceed the sum of the uncertainties of the premises divided by the probability of the conditional's antecedent. Hence we can say roughly that if a truth-conditionally sound inference with conditional conclusion has highly probable premises then its conclusion must be probable *provided the conditional's antecedent is not highly improbable.* Plausible hypothesis: recognition that a conclusion's antecedent is not too improbable is a 'tacit premise' in much real life reasoning which appears to be of a pattern which is not universally probabilistically sound. The application of this to contraposition and the inference of a conditional from a disjunction will be considered in a moment. Note first, though, that if 'recognition of non-improbability' is to be taken as a tacit premise of reasoning of the kinds we are considering, then these premises cannot be expressed within any standard logical symbolism, and it is possible that systematic analysis of reasoning involving them will require not only a semantic generalization of standard logic, but a syntactic one as well.

Now consider the inference of the conditional from the disjunction:

$$\frac{A \vee B}{- A \Rightarrow B}.$$

Combining earlier generalities we get:

$$u\left(- A \Rightarrow B\right) = \frac{u\left(A \vee B\right)}{u\left(A\right)},$$

hence the conclusion's uncertainty will be low if the premise uncertainty is low and $u(A)$ is not too low. It is plausible that in the usual situation in which one *considers* disjunctions and what follows from them, their first disjuncts will by themselves be 'fairly uncertain', hence in those situations it will be rational to infer a conditional from them.

Look a bit deeper and consider the situation in which a hearer is *told* a proposition of the form $A \vee B$. Let us assume that the hearer is justified in believing what he is told, and therefore he may attach as high a probability to $A \vee B$ as the speaker himself does. It is also plausible that it is *misleading* (though not false) for a speaker to make a disjunctive assertion where he is in a position to assert one of the disjuncts. Thus, when the speaker asserts $A \vee B$ he cannot assert A by itself since it is too uncertain, and so he should also regard $-A \Rightarrow B$ as probable. Hearers having reason to accept $A \vee B$ when they are told it therefore have reason to think the speaker might also have told them $-A \Rightarrow B$, and plausibly have as good reason to accept that as to accept the explicitly asserted disjunction. This 'conversationally implied conditional' (to borrow Grice's terminology [26] as well as his analytical approach) is, however, one which may be 'cancelled', which shows that the implication of the conditional is not 'part of the meaning' of the disjunction. Thus, a speaker may cancel by saying "I know which one of A and B is the case but I will only tell you that one of them is." In such circumstances the hearer would be justified in concluding $A \vee B$ but not in inferring $-A \Rightarrow B$ (because it is not improbable that the speaker says what he says only because he knows that A is the case, and this would not allow the inference to $-A \Rightarrow B$).

Two comments on the foregoing are in order. First, our explanation of the rationality of inferring $-A \Rightarrow B$ when one is told $A \vee B$ puts the disjunction in an unusual light, since it suggests that disjunctions are misleadingly *asserted* by speakers who *know* that they are true in virtue of knowing one of the disjuncts. This runs directly counter to the Intuitionistic theory of the disjunction according to which it is to be asserted only if a disjunct is known (Heyting [31], p. 24). At any rate, we are here confronted with a divergence between what it is proper to *say* without running serious risk of misleading hearers, and what it is rational to *think*. Probability, we would argue, is directly relevant to the latter, but only incidental to the former.

The second comment is that both Grice [26] and Lewis [40] use conversational implicature considerations to prove the opposite of what we have just argued for: i.e., to prove that the 'if... then...' of ordinary English is *logically* the material conditional, and that irrationalities like the fallacies of material implication are to be explained on the basis of violations of laws of conversational implicature. It is well known that conversational implicatures are extremely difficult to distinguish from logical consequences, and at the present juncture the author's conclusions as to what is part of the meanings of $A \vee B$ and $-A \Rightarrow B$ and what is just conversationally implied by utterance of statements of these forms simply disagree with Grice's and Lewis's conclusions concerning these questions. How to decide who is right? Even Grice's tests concerning what can be 'cancelled' may be argued both ways. For now we must simply adopt a position consonent with our ratio representation of the probability of the conditional, according to which it is in some sense 'part of the meaning of' the indicative conditional that its probability is appropriately measured as a conditional probability, and which implicitly contradicts the conclusions of Grice and Lewis. Chapter III attempts to deal with these matters, though even there nothing will be conclusively settled.

Similar comments may be made about the contraposition schema. The uncertainty of the conclusion $A \Rightarrow -B$ cannot exceed the uncertainty of the premise $B \Rightarrow -A$ divided by the probability of A, hence it will be rational to accept the conclusion 'given' the premise unless $p(A)$ is too small and $p(-A)$ is too great. But in the ordinary situation in which a speaker makes an assertion of the form $B \Rightarrow -A$ it is plausible that it is unusual for $-A$ to be by itself probable. Possibly it is misleading and in violation of conversational 'helpfulness maxims' for a speaker to say, e.g. "if Jones attends the party then Smith won't" when he also believes "Smith won't attend the party." In such circumstances one feels the 'even if' locution to be the appropriate one, as in "Smith won't attend the party, even if Jones attends" or "there won't be a terrific cloudburst, even if it rains."[9] Granted this, it would follow by an argument analogous to one applying to inferences of conditionals from disjunctions that hearers are justified by conversational implicatures in contraposing and inferring $A \Rightarrow -B$ when speakers make statements of the form $B \Rightarrow -A$. Note that while contraposition and conditional inversion stand on all fours as regards purely probabilistic soundness, the same conversational implicatures which justify the inference of $A \Rightarrow -B$ in situations where one is told $B \Rightarrow -A$ do not justify inverting and inferring $B \Rightarrow A$ when one is told $A \Rightarrow B$ (though it is arguable that being told $A \Rightarrow B$ should increase the probability of $B \Rightarrow A$).

5. THE HYPOTHETICAL SYLLOGISM AND ASPECTS OF HYPOTHETICAL REASONING

The rationality of apparent instances of such *Hypothetical Syllogism* inferences as

> If Jones studies he will pass. If he passes he will graduate. Therefore, if he studies he will graduate.

is not plausibly explained by reference to conversational implicatures, and we now suggest that the right way to view reasoning of this sort is to regard the second premise as elliptical. More exactly, we suggest that the 'hypothesis' of the first premise (the antecedent of the conditional) is tacitly 'presupposed' in the second, and analysis of the reasoning requires that this presupposition be made explicit as in:

> If Jones studies he will pass. If he passes (still supposing he studied) he will graduate. Therefore, if he studies he will graduate.

We will not attempt a rigorous justification of the foregoing intuitively plausible suggestion, but we will now see that if the suggestion is correct it would explain why apparent Hypothetical Syllogism inferences are rational, and also see that the suggestion links Hypothetical Syllogisms in a natural way to certain kinds of hypothetical reasoning from *assumptions*, and related inference patterns.

Observe first that what is wrong in the Smith-Jones election counter-instance to the Hypothetical Syllogism cited in Section 3 is just that its second premise cannot be 'restricted' by adding the hypothesis of the first premise to its antecedent. Making this restriction would in fact yield an inference with an absurd second premise:

> If Smith dies before the election then Jones will win. If Jones wins (still supposing Smith died before the election) then Smith will retire after the election. Therefore, if Smith dies before the election he will retire after the election.

Second, we will see in Chapter II that making the tacit presupposition of the second premise of a real life Hypothetical Syllogism explicit transforms it into an instance of the *Restricted Hypothetical Syllogism* pattern

$$\frac{A \Rightarrow B, (A \ \& \ B) \Rightarrow C}{A \Rightarrow C},$$

which is universally probabilistically sound in that the uncertainty of its conclusion can never exceed the sum of the uncertainties of its premises. Thus, our suggestion is that when apparent Hypothetical Syllogisms are properly analyzed as Restricted Hypothetical Syllogisms, it is not necessary to inquire further into their conditions of partial soundness since such inferences are universally sound. Conversely, purported counter-instances to the Hypothetical Syllogism are in a sense 'unrealistic' because they do not transform to Restricted Hypothetical Syllogisms in the ordinary way. Of course, this does not mean that it is not important to recognize that real life Hypothetical Syllogisms are elliptical (assuming this is so), for failure to recognize this makes the development of an adequate theory of such reasoning very difficult.

Very similar remarks can be made about the partial inverse to the Antecedent Restriction pattern

$$\frac{(A \& B) \Rightarrow C, A}{B \Rightarrow C}$$

mentioned in Section 3. Though this pattern is not universally sound, apparent instances of it are very common, as in:

> If the President and Secretary are present, the meeting can begin. The President is present. Therefore, if the Secretary is present the meeting can begin.

As with the Hypothetical Syllogism, it is plausible that in reasoning of this sort the second premise is elliptical, and making a tacit presupposition explicit transforms it to:

> If the President and Secretary are present the meeting can begin. The President is present (even if the Secretary is present). Therefore if the Secretary is present the meeting can begin.

This transforms the inference to the form

$$\frac{(A \& B) \Rightarrow C, A \text{ (even if })}{B \Rightarrow C} \quad \text{or} \quad \frac{(A \& B) \Rightarrow C, A, B \Rightarrow A}{B \Rightarrow C}$$

which is universally probabilistically sound since it is in fact a special case of the Restricted Hypothetical Syllogism.

Hypothesizing that apparent instances of Hypothetical Syllogisms and related forms are elliptical and involve tacit suppositions suggests a close connection between this type of reasoning and certain kinds of *hypothetical reasoning* from suppositions or assumptions, such as in the following example of a *Conditional Proof*:

> Suppose the Dodgers don't win the pennant. Then the Reds
> will win the pennant. If the Reds win the pennant they will not
> win the World Series. So, if the Dodgers don't win the pennant,
> the National League team will not win the World Series.

Our suggestion is that this reasoning is not properly analyzed by regarding
the initial supposition as an independent 'premise', but rather by regarding the supposition as a prior 'formulation' of a hypothesis which is
common to a series of succeeding conditionals and which it is convenient
to formulate once at the outset rather than repeatedly. Thus analyzed,
the above reasoning is to be regarded as having the same force as:

> If the Dodgers don't win the pennant then the Reds will. If the
> Reds win the pennant (still supposing the Dodgers don't) they
> won't win the World Series. So, if the Dodgers don't win the
> pennant the National League team will not win the World
> Series.

Here we have something very close to a Restricted Hypothetical Syllogism.

Our suggested reduction of Conditional Proof to reasoning without
'assumptions' is of course no more than an application of the steps used
in proving the Deduction Theorem to real life reasoning of the Conditional Proof pattern. This reduction takes on an added importance in the
real life application, however, because it is the key to applying probabilistic analysis to such reasoning. Two facts should be noted: (1) Conditional
Proof is not universally probabilistically sound, and (2) the direct application of our probabilistic soundness criterion only makes sense where the
premises of the inferences in question are *accepted* propositions, and does
not make sense where 'premises' include 'assumptions' or 'entertained
but not accepted propositions.' To show that Conditional Proof is not
always probabilistically sound it is sufficient to note that if it *were* sound
it would be possible to derive the fallacious pattern

$$\frac{B}{A \Rightarrow B}.$$

Thus, accepting B and assuming A, B would follow, and therefore $A \Rightarrow B$
should follow from B alone by Conditional Proof. On the other hand, the
very fact that persons commonly appear to reason after the Conditional

Proof pattern suggests that such reasoning ordinarily *is* sound, and the way to analyze its conditions of soundness is reveal its 'deep structure' by transforming it to reasoning involving only accepted propositions (as in the baseball example). The details of such an analysis remain to be worked out, and this matter will not be pursued farther here, since we are concerned in this book primarily with *direct* inference.

Finally, we may wonder whether the technique of reduction to direct inference (not involving assumptions) for the purpose of applying probabilistic analysis will work in the case of other familiar patterns of indirect reasoning. We would conjecture that such a reduction *will* work in the case of Proof by Cases (used in reasoning from premises of disjunctive form, where each disjunct is 'assumed' in order in arriving at a conclusion), but not in the case of *Reductio ad Absurdum*. The special problem which arises in the *Reductio* case is that the propositions involved are generally expressed in the subjunctive or *counterfactual* mood, and reduction to direct inference would lead to counterfactual conditionals. These are known to involve special difficulties, and we will see in Chapter IV that to the extent to which probabilistic analysis applies to them at all, it is in a much more complicated way than in its application to indicatives.

6. THE SCOPE OF ANTECEDENT RESTRICTABILITY

It was noted in Section 3 that the Antecedent Restriction schema

$$\frac{B \Rightarrow C}{(A \mathbin{\&} B) \Rightarrow C}$$

is only partially sound, and in this section we will be concerned with those propositions A which can be conjoined with the antecedents of accepted conditionals $B \Rightarrow C$ (on particular occasions) without rendering them improbable or unacceptable. Roughly, let us call the class of propositions A which can be conjoined with the antecedent of an accepted (sufficiently probable) conditional $B \Rightarrow C$ without rendering it unacceptable on an occasion the *scope of antecedent restrictability*, or, more briefly, the *scope* of the conditional on the occasion. The intuitive significance of the scope of an accepted or asserted conditional is that it comprises those factual propositions which are *probabilistically compatible* with the conditional in the sense that coming to accept such a proposition as a certainty would not lead to retracting the original conditional (matters of retraction in the light of new information will be taken up in Chapter IV).

Inequality (3) below gives useful information about the scope of an accepted conditional $B \Rightarrow C$:

$$(3) \qquad u((A \& B) \Rightarrow C) \leqslant \frac{u(B \Rightarrow C)}{p(B \Rightarrow A)}$$

(note the resemblance to Equation (1) where an uncertainty is divided by a probability on the right). An immediate consequence of (3) is that the more probable $B \Rightarrow C$ is the broader its scope will be, and if $B \Rightarrow C$ is *certain* then its scope will be *universal* in the sense that all factual propositions will be included (though complications can arise here when the presently disregarded cases of zero antecedent probability are taken into account). This is a reflection of the fact that the more certain a proposition is, the less likely it is to be overthrown by new evidence.

Any proposition A such that $p(A \Rightarrow B)$ is not too low will belong to the scope of $B \Rightarrow C$, but this fact may be generalized and put into perspective as follows. Note first that the concept of *scope* can be extended to cover accepted factual propositions C by the device of regarding C as the consequent of a conditional $B \Rightarrow C$ with tautologous antecedent B. What was said above about conditionals then applies to factual propositions as well: the more probable they are the larger their scopes are, and when they are certain their scopes are universal. We may also add the following which is true of factual but not of all conditional propositions: any accepted factual proposition includes any other accepted factual proposition in its scope. Figuratively, the scope of an accepted factual proposition includes the 'accepted world' (the class of all other factual propositions accepted on the same occasion). This generalizes to certain conditional propositions.

What was said about conditionals' scopes at the beginning of the previous paragraph can be restated as follows: the scope of an accepted conditional $B \Rightarrow C$ includes all factual propositions A which include the conditional's antecedent, B, in their scopes. Any proposition B which is not too improbable will belong to the scope of all accepted factual propositions A, and therefore if B is not too improbable an accepted conditional $B \Rightarrow C$ must also include all accepted A in its scope – its scope includes the accepted world. Generalizing, we can say that the more probable B is, the larger the scope of accepted $B \Rightarrow C$ will be, and the more probable A is, the more likely it will be to be in the scope of $B \Rightarrow C$. In particular, if A is certain it will certainly belong to the scope even of somewhat uncertain $B \Rightarrow C$ – the scope of conditional $B \Rightarrow C$ must include the 'known world' (the class of all propositions known as certainties). Summing up: a conditional proposition's scope always includes the known world and will include the accepted world if its antecedent is not too improbable – and factual propositions can be regarded as conditionals with 'not too improbable' (tautologous) antecedents.

Various other properties of scope might be examined, but we will conclude here by noting that this concept can be generalized to apply to other conditionals like material and counterfactual conditionals as well, and that this generalization provides an interesting way of comparing them. Let Cond (B, C) be any kind of accepted conditional; then A can be said to belong to the scope of Cond (B, C) on some occasion if Cond $(A \, \& \, B, C)$ is also acceptable on that occasion. Though this generalized notion of scope can no longer be identified with the class of propositions which are probabilistically compatible with conditionals other than indicatives, the following may be noted. The scope of an accepted material conditional is always *universal* since $p((A \, \& \, B) \supset C)$ is always at least as high as $p(B \supset C)$. The scope of an indicative conditional is only universal if it is perfectly certain, but it always includes the *known* world (all propositions with probability 1), and it includes the accepted world (all propositions which are 'sufficiently probable') if its antecedent is not too improbable. We will see in Chapter IV that the counterfactual's scope usually includes *less* than the known world, and in fact includes all of the known world only if it coincides with the corresponding indicative conditional. More generally, we will find systematic ambiguities in the counterfactual which are ultimately traceable to ambiguities in their scopes, and which can only be resolved 'contextually'.

For now, however, we are concerned only with indicative conditionals, and the thing to be kept in mind is that the scope of a conditional defines the conditions of partial rationality of Antecedent Restriction inferences involving it, which depends primarily on two things: (1) the certainty of the conditional, and (2) the certainty of the propositions which can be conjoined with the conditional's antecedent. The next section examines

another kind of Antecedent Restriction inference, which involves an un-
doubted anomaly in the applicability of our theory.

7. A DIFFICULTY ABOUT CONDITIONALS
WITH DISJUNCTIVE ANTECEDENTS

We pause briefly in this section to consider a difficulty which is most
easily, if superficially, disposed of as a problem of formalization. This arises in the analysis of the 'disjunctive restriction' inference pattern

$$\frac{(A \vee B) \Rightarrow C}{B \Rightarrow C} .$$

which is formally just a trivial variation on the 'conjunctive' restriction
pattern already discussed. As with the previously discussed pattern it is
easy to construct a Venn Diagram representing the premise as highly
probable (because most of the union of A and B lies inside C) while the
conclusion is improbable (because most of B lies outside C). Figure 6
below depicts such a probabilistic state of affairs:

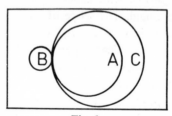

Fig. 6.

Our problem arises in attempting to translate the probabilistic relations
represented in the diagram into a concrete counter-instance to the schema.
It is required to find propositions A, B, and C such that: (1) B is much less
probable than A, (2) A probabilistically entails C, and (3) B and C
'exclude' one another. The three propositions below, drawn from our
Smith-Jones election example, fit these requirements:

$$B = \text{Smith will die before the election.}$$
$$A = \text{Jones will win the election.}$$
$$C = \text{Smith will retire after the election.}$$

However, when these propositions are substituted for '*B*', '*A*', and '*C*', respectively, in the schema, instead of arriving at a highly probable premise and a highly improbable conclusion we end with an inference whose premise is absurd:

> If either Jones wins the election or Smith dies before it then Smith will retire. Therefore, if Smith dies before the election he will retire.

At the heart of the difficulty above is the fact that while according to the laws of probability we have assumed until now the premise is probable, nevertheless the premise is intuitively absurd. Nor is this intuitive absurdity to be explained in terms of conversational implicatures. Such an explanation would entail that the inference of "if *B* then *C*" from the premise "if either *A* or *B* then *C*" was justified by a conversational implicature which was not part of the meaning of the English expression "if either *A* or *B* then *C*". But *this* implication cannot be 'cancelled' in the way it is possible to signal the impropriety of the hearer's inferring the contrapositive, without at the same time rendering the original affirmation unintelligible.

In the light of the foregoing, we must conclude that it is inappropriate to apply probability measures in the standard way to propositions expressible in English in the form "if either *A* or *B* then *C*". For completeness' sake, however, we will continue to use the symbolism '$(A \vee B) \Rightarrow C$', and to attach probabilities to such formulas in the way we have previously done. The consequence, though, is that we must avoid symbolizing "if either *A* or *B* then *C*" as '$(A \vee B) \Rightarrow C$', and must analyze reasoning involving the former in some other way. Admittedly this is hardly desirable in work which aims to improve on orthodox logic's excessive preoccupation with formalism to the neglect of application, but in mitigation it is possible to suggest a way of analyzing reasoning involving "if either *A* or *B* then *C*" within the probabilistic framework. This is to treat this expression as having the same logical force as the conjunction "if *A* then *C and* if *B* then *C*." We cannot symbolize the transformed form directly since it involves a conjunction of conditionals and these are not included in our formalism (because probabilities do not apply to them, and we want to avoid formulas to which probabilities don't attach). However, whenever 'if either *A* or *B* then *C*' appears as a premise, then this premise can be symbolized by the addition of *two* premises $A \Rightarrow C$ and $B \Rightarrow C$ to the other premises of the reasoning.

Two concluding remarks may be made on issues connected with conditionals with disjunctive antecedents. First, our proposal to represent "if A or B then C" as the conjunction "if A then C and if B then C" for purposes of logical analysis allows us to avoid another problem about these forms: namely that they appear to violate the principal of inter-substitutability of logical equivalents. If we agree that the two statements

> Jones will win.

and

> Either Smith won't die before the election and Jones will win or Smith will die before the election and Jones will win.

are logically equivalent, then it should follow from the inter-substitutability principal that the conditionals

> If Jones wins then Smith will retire.

and

> If either Smith doesn't die before the election and Jones wins or Smith does die before the election and Jones wins, then Smith will retire.

were equivalent. However, the first is very probable while the second is absurd. The proposal to read the latter as a conjunction of conditionals avoids the difficulty by treating conditionals whose antecedents are of the grammatical form of disjunctions as being in reality of a different logical form. This is not entirely satisfactory of course, since we would still like to know *why* the disjunctive grammatical form is employed if it is not 'logically meant.' This must be left as an unsolved problem for now, however.

The second remark concerns forms related to the conditional with disjunctive antecedent, and especially the *only if* construction. Consider the proposition

> Jones will win only if he draws an ace.

The standard logical analysis is to treat this as equivalent to

> If Jones doesn't draw an ace then he won't win.

However a plausibly better paraphrase should replace the antecedent "Jones won't draw an ace" by the superficially equivalent "Jones will draw a 2 or draw a three or..." so that the 'only if' gets analyzed as a conditional with a disjunctive antecedent:

> If Jones draws a 2 or draws a 3 or... (anything besides an ace) then he won't win.

And, according to our suggested reading of conditionals with disjunctive antecedents, this is to be construed logically as a conjunction

> If Jones draws a 2 he won't win, and if he draws a 3 he won't win, etc.

The upshot of this proposal is that *only if* is not to be treated as a 'simple' conditional construction, and in consequence we are not to apply a single numerical probability to propositions like "Jones will win only if he gets an ace".

The next section discusses the general problem of dealing with compounds like conjunctions with conditional conjuncts within our probabilistic framework.

8. The Problem of Compounds of Conditionals

It is a drawback to our probabilistic approach in comparison to the usual truth-functional one that it does not provide us with a theory of inferences involving compound propositions with conditional constituents, whereas truth-conditional logic does provide such a theory. We shall shortly see that there are serious difficulties to confront in extending probabilistic analysis to these problematic propositions and inferences involving them, but we want to argue first that it is a somewhat dubious 'advantage' to the truth-conditional approach that it does apply to such inferences. The application is a very poor one, and it might be much better to frankly admit that at present we don't understand such constructions rather than to delude ourselves with a very inadequate theory. A few examples of misapplication are given below, which it is hoped that the reader will recognize as typical. More systematic survey of these inferences is out of place here, since forthcoming work by William Cooper [12] investigates these matters in detail.

First consider denials of conditionals, which notoriously fail to conform to the tenets of truth-conditional theory. Thus, truth-conditional logic would hold the following to be sound:

> It is not the case that if it rains then the exercises will be held indoors. Therefore, it will rain.

This fallacy is well known, and the only thing to be noted about it here is that it is the inverse of the fallacy of material implication

> It will not rain. Therefore, if it rains the exercises will be held indoors.

It is somewhat odd that there are many to be found who defend the rationality of the latter inference, though the former is almost without exception condemned as irrational.

Turning to disjunctions with conditional components, there are many problems. One is that the form "either A or if A then B" is a tautology when analyzed truth-conditionally, hence it should be acceptable no matter what. However, it is not evident that one would want to maintain

> Either it will rain or if it rains the exercises will be held indoors.

under any circumstances, particularly in view of the fact that both disjuncts can be extremely improbable at the same time. Of course, the non-tautologousness of this form is closely connected with the fact that the inference of $A \Rightarrow B$ from $-A$ is not always sound.

A related fallacy is the inference of "either $A \Rightarrow C$ or $B \Rightarrow C$" from $(A \& B) \Rightarrow C$, which is truth-conditionally sound but often absurd as in:

> If switches A and B are thrown the motor will start. Therefore, either if switch A is thrown the motor will start or if switch B is thrown the motor will start.

(this example originally appeared in [1]). Again, the absurdity becomes manifest when we recall that the premise can be arbitrarily highly probable while *both* disjuncts in the conclusion are simultaneously arbitrarily improbable.

Conjunctions of conditionals cause no special problems for truth-conditional logic, but by the same token they present no difficulties for probabilistic analysis so long as they are treated as *joint assertions* where probabilities attach to the individual conjuncts and not to the conjunction as a whole.

One might anticipate difficulties with conditionals which contain other conditionals in their *antecedents*, and the following example bears this out:

> If it is the case that if Jones studies he will pass logic, then he will pass logic. Therefore, if Jones doesn't study he will pass logic.

Pity poor Jones if he learns logic so well as to begin to reason in this way![10] Conditionals with other conditionals in their consequents would seem less problematical because of the intuitive plausibility of the equivalence of $A \Rightarrow (B \Rightarrow C)$ and $(A \& B) \Rightarrow C$. Nonetheless, acceptance of this equivalence would entail giving up *Modus Ponens* in application to conditionals with conditional consequents. Thus, $(A \& B) \Rightarrow A$ is a tautology which should be acceptable no matter what, and the equivalence would then imply that $A \Rightarrow (B \Rightarrow A)$ should also be acceptable no matter what. If *Modus Ponens* were valid, then we should always infer $B \Rightarrow A$ from A together with the universally acceptable $A \Rightarrow (B \Rightarrow A)$. But we know independently that this inference is not always sound.

What of the possibility of extending probabilistic analysis directly to compounds of conditionals by defining suitable measures of the probabilities of these compounds? We might be warned by the fact that probability theory does not use such measures that there should be difficulties in principal in the way of effecting such an extension, and David Lewis' *triviality result* [40] can be viewed as showing clearly what those difficulties are. Before considering Lewis' own argument, though, it is to be noted that the straightforward extension of probability to compounds of conditionals stands or falls with the possibility of defining truth for simple conditionals in such a way that probability will equal probability of truth. Obviously if probability could be equated with probability of truth in the case on uncompounded conditionals, there would be no problem about defining the probabilities of compounds like conjunctions of conditionals; i.e., as the probability that both conjuncts are true. Conversely, suppose probabilities could be applied to both conjunctions and denials of conditionals in such a way as to satisfy the usual axioms (e.g. that the probability of a disjunction of inconsistent propositions equals the sum of the probabilities of the disjuncts). Then probabilities would apply to Carnapian *state descriptions* with conditional constituents, which would act formally like possible states of affairs, and probabilities of simple conditionals would then equal the sums of the probabilities of of the possible states of affairs in which they were true. That is, probability could be equated to probability of truth, which we know is not possible if the assumptions outlined in Section 2 are satisfied. Lewis' argument, the key steps of which are restated below, makes the foregoing heuristic argument precise.

Using the standard conditional probability notation, $p(\ /\ )$, suppose this function defined for all pairs of propositions, *including conditionals* such that the second member of the pair has positive probability. Suppose further that this conditional probability function satisfies the usual axioms, and that *probabilities change by conditionalization* – after learning A the unconditional probability of B should equal the original conditional probability $p(B/A)$. Finally, suppose that probabilities of conditionals are conditional probabilities: $p(A \Rightarrow B) = p(B/A)$. Assuming that probabilities change by conditionalization it would then follow that for any C such that $p(A\ \&\ C)$ is positive,

$$p(A \Rightarrow B/C) = p(B/A\ \&\ C)$$

This follows in virtue of the fact that $p(A \Rightarrow B/C)$ should equal the unconditional probability $p(A \Rightarrow B)$ after C is learned, and this in turn should equal $p(B/A)$ after C is learned.

Two special cases of the above equation are those in which C equals B and in which C is $-B$. Assuming that both $p(A\ \&\ B)$ and $p(A\ \&\ -B)$ are positive, it would follow from the usual laws that

$$p(A \Rightarrow B/B) = 1$$

and

$$p(A \Rightarrow B/-B) = 0.$$

By the definition of conditional probability, however, $p(A \Rightarrow B/B) = p((A \Rightarrow B)\ \&\ B)/p(B)$, from which it would follow since the left side of the equation equals 1 and $p(B)$ is not zero that

$$p((A \Rightarrow B)\ \&\ B) = p(B).$$

An analogous argument yields the conclusion that

$$p((A \Rightarrow B)\ \&\ -B) = 0.$$

Finally, by standard laws of probability,

$$p(A \Rightarrow B) = p((A \Rightarrow B) \& B) + p((A \Rightarrow B) \& -B)$$
$$= p(B).$$

In effect, A and B must be statistically independent no matter what A and B are, so long as both $p(A \& B)$ and $p(A \& -B)$ are both positive! It is now a simple matter to show that the only way this 'universal independence' could hold would be for there to be only four possible probability values.

Close examination of Lewis' argument shows it to rest on four distinct assumptions, and as in the case of possible reactions to the earlier argument concerning the possibility of equating probability with probability of truth in the case of conditionals, reactions to the triviality argument depend on which of these assumptions is abandoned or modified. The assumptions are: (1) probabilities of unconditional propositions satisfy the usual (Kolmogorov) axioms, (2) probabilities of simple conditionals are conditional probabilities, (3) probabilities attach to truth-conditional compounds (in particular conjunctions) of conditionals in such a way as to satisfy the Kolmogorov axioms, (4) probabilities change by conditionalization. As noted in Section 2, Lewis himself gives up (2), van Fraassen gives up (4), and Skyrms proposes modifying (3) by attaching something like probabilistic 'values' to compounds of conditionals which, however, do not satisfy all of the usual laws. Lewis' argument shows that the difficulty in attaching probabilities to compounds of conditionals arises with almost the simplest of such compounds, namely those of the forms $p((A \Rightarrow B) \& B)$ and $p((A \Rightarrow B) \& -B)$, which the usual laws of probability would require to sum to $p(A \Rightarrow B)$ but which would apparently entail that $p(A \Rightarrow B)$ should equal $p(B)$. The author's very tentative opinion on the 'right way out' of the triviality argument is that we should regard the inapplicability of probability to compounds of conditionals as a fundamental limitation of probability, on a par with the inapplicability of truth to simple conditionals. What is needed at the present stage is less mathematical theorizing than close examination of the phenomena of inference involving these problematic constructions, where it is conceivable that an adequate theory will ultimately require just as radical a departure from the probabilistic 'conceptual scheme' as this scheme is itself radically different from the orthodox truth-conditional viewpoint.

Even granting the difficulties of applying probabilities directly to compounds of conditionals, it is still possible to learn something about inference patterns involving these constructions by considering possible probabilities of their 'probabilistic components' – i.e., the components to which probabilities do apply. Confining attention here only to uniterated truth-conditional compounds of conditionals (excluding both conditionals of conditionals and such things as negations of conjunctions of conditionals), there are no special problems with conjunctions since they can be treated as joint assertions. There are strong forces suggesting the appropriateness of treating at least one reading of the denial of $A \Rightarrow B$ as the conditional denial, $A \Rightarrow -B$, some of which will be discussed in the next section. This leaves disjunction as it might occur in the inference:

> Jones will pass logic. Therefore, either if he studies he will pass logic, or, if he doesn't study he will pass logic.

What can probability tell us about the above inference? At least this much: the *sum* of the probabilities of the disjuncts in the conclusion must be at least as great as the probability of the premise. The satisfaction of this requirement shows that the inference satisfies at least a *necessary* condition for soundness: namely that it should not be possible for the premise to highly probable while *both* disjuncts in the conclusion are highly improbable (which was possible in the 'switches' example). The foregoing also shows that the inference satisfies a generalization of a necessary and sufficient condition for an inference with a factual disjunctive conclusion to be sound: namely that the premise together with the denial (or conditional denial) of either disjunct should entail the other disjunct. Whether we are willing to take this as showing that it is rational to accept any disjunction of the form $(A \Rightarrow B) \vee (-A \Rightarrow B)$ on the basis of B depends on further considerations which it may possibly lie beyond the bounds of probability to deal with.

Similar considerations apply to inferences with disjunctions of conditionals among their premises such as the patterns:

$$\frac{(A \Rightarrow B) \vee (A \Rightarrow C)}{A \Rightarrow (B \vee C)} \qquad \frac{(A \Rightarrow C) \vee (-A \Rightarrow C)}{C} \, .$$

The first pattern is one such that the inference of the conclusion from either disjunct of the premise is sound, and if this is taken as it is in the factual case as a necessary and sufficient condition for the conclusion to be entailed by the disjunction, then the inference should be sound. In the second inference, the conclusion is entailed by neither disjunct of the premises, and this suggests that the inference should be unsound. The probabilistic meaning of the foregoing is that the conclusion of the first inference could not be highly improbable without both disjuncts of the premise being at best 50% probable, while the conclusion of the second inference could be highly improbable while a disjunct of its first premise was almost a certainty. Again, whether we want to take these facts as *establishing* the soundness of the first inference pattern and the unsoundness of the second will depend on a deeper analysis of the disjunction of the conditional construction.

9. A PROBABILISTIC CONCEPT OF CONSISTENCY: DENIALS AND CONTRARIES OF CONDITIONALS

Though we will be concerned with the concept of consistency in this book largely for technical reasons, this section will consider a probabilistic explanation of intuitive inconsistency in relation to conditional propositions which in turn motivates a definition of *probabilistic consistency* whose technical aspects will be explored in the next chapter. There are fallacies of consistency which arise in applying standard logic in determining the consistency of sets of propositions involving conditionals, and which may be regarded as the 'consistency-theoretic' counterparts of the fallacies of material implication. Two very simple examples of proposition-sets which are held to be consistent in current theory but which are intuitively inconsistent are:

> If it rains the game will be postponed.
> If it rains the game won't be postponed.

and the *conditional self-contradiction*

> If it rains then it won't rain.[11]

Truth-conditional semanticists might claim that ordinary logic's 'error' in holding these proposition-sets to be consistent (assuming it is an error) stems from its mistaken application of material conditional truth-values to 'real' conditionals, but if we are right in holding that truth-values don't even *apply* to conditionals, then the explanation of the inconsistency in these examples is not to be sought in terms of incompatible truth-conditions according to the usual logical definition of inconsistency, and what is needed is a reexamination of the concept of consistency itself.

A plausible explanation of the intuitive inconsistency of the propositions in the examples consists in observing that it would be irrational to *accept* all propositions in an inconsistent set at once, because in fact it is not possible for all propositions of the set to be simultaneously probable. Our probabilistic analysis supports this intuition since it follows from the conditional probability representation that the two propositions "if it rains the game will be postponed" and "if it rains the game won't be postponed" cannot simultaneously be more than 50% probable, and the single proposition "if it rains then it won't rain" must always have probability 0. It is true that this ignores problems having to do with the possibility that the antecedent "it will rain" might have probability 0, which will be considered briefly below, but at least we can say that the propositions in question cannot be simultaneously probable if there is a non-zero probability of rain. Thus, probabilistic analysis permits a very natural explanation of intuitive inconsistency in non-truth-conditionals terms, which links it to what it is not rational to accept.

Building on the foregoing explanation of the intuitive inconsistency of propositions like "if it rains then it won't rain", we may propose a rough definition of *probabilistic consistency* as follows: a proposition or set of propositions is probabilistically consistent if and only if it is possible for the proposition to be highly probable, or for all propositions of the set to be highly probable at once. The probabilistic definition can be regarded as the 'probabilistic transform' of the standard truth-conditional definition of consistency, which arises when the phrase 'highly probable' is substituted throughout for the word 'true' in the latter. It is also easily seen that, so long as there are not 'too many' propositions in the set under consideration, the probabilistic concept reduces to the truth-conditional one in application to sets of factual propositions. This helps to explain why truth-conditional tests of consistency yield results in fair agreement with intuition in application to *factual* proposition-sets. It turns out furthermore that when the concept of probabilistic consistency is given a suitable precization it is linked to the idea of universal probabilistic soundness in a very simple way: this is that an inference schema is universally probabilistically sound if and only if the premises of the schema are probabilistically inconsistent with the *contrary* of the conclusion. Thus, something like a generalization of *Reductio ad Absurdum* holds for arguments involving conditionals, provided that contraries of conclusions are treated as denials. Most important technically is the fact that it is frequently convenient to approach the problem of determining universal probabilistic soundness by reducing it to one of determining probabilistic consistency. In fact, this is the approach which will be followed in the next chapter, where the study of probabilistic consistency is a preliminary to that of probabilistic soundness.

Let us return briefly to the matter of justifying the 'contraries' reading of "it is not the case that if A then B." There seem to be several logical forces supporting this interpretation, among which the following may be cited. (1) This agrees reasonably well with intuition. (2) The interpretation allows an attractive escape from the standard logical dilemma of maintaining that "it is not the case that if A then B" entails A and 'not B'. (3) At least when $P(A)$ is non-zero, P (if A then not B) is 1 minus P (if A then B), which is the same relation as that in which the probabilities of factual propositions and their denials stand. Finally, we have just seen that this interpretation permits us to generalize the truth-conditional connection between inconsistency and logical consequence in an elegant manner. One is almost inclined to say that if denials of conditionals are not their contraries, then they ought to be.

In spite of, or perhaps because of the foregoing we must be especially on guard against allowing the desire for theoretical elegance to blind us to messy realities in the phenomena which the theories are supposed to describe. At any rate, there is an obvious alternative to the contraries reading of conditional denial which may well be the more common one in ordinary discourse. This is the *non-justification* sense of denial (which also applies to non-conditional denial) which is often meant when someone says "that is not the case" in explicit rejection of another person's affirmation. Roughly translated into probabilistic terms, this sense of "it is not the case that if it rains the game will be postponed" does not mean that it is highly probable that if it rains the game won't be postponed (the 'contraries' reading) but rather that it is not highly probable that if it rains the game will be postponed. Of course, if the "it is not the case that" locution really has the two clearly distinguishable senses we have suggested, we might argue that all that is needed is disambiguation in particular contexts so that we know just how reasoning involving this form of denial is to be evaluated.

Two points are worth making about the non-justification sense of denial in application to conditionals. First, unlike the contraries reading which *can* be expressed in our 'object language' formalism, there is no way of expressing the non-justification sense of denial within this formalism. This is because we have no operation which carries formulas into 'non-justification denials' which have the property that the original formula is highly probable if and only if its non-justification denial is not highly probable. Whether or not it would be possible to enrich our formalism in such a way as to include symbolizations of non-justification denials without at the same time running up against difficulties like those shown in the triviality results is an open question. The second point is that the non-justification sense of denial is closely related to the alternative reading of conditional disjunction mentioned in the last section, which was, roughly, that "either if A then B or if A then C" can be read as "one of the two conditionals is highly probable" (though it may not be known which). The alternative readings of both denial and disjunction are expressed 'metalinguistically' as sentential compounds of statements *about* the probabilities of object language expressions which have no object language counterparts.

Finally, honesty compels us to acknowledge the inconclusiveness of much of what we have said both about inconsistency and denial in application to conditionals, which arises from our neglect of the possibility that the antecedents of the conditionals involved may have zero probability and we have no theory which applies to that case. Are we really entitled to say that "if A then B" and "if A then not B" cannot be simultaneously probable if we don't know what probabilities these propositions should have in case $P(A)$ is 0? As a matter of fact, in my earlier articles [1] and [2] I arbitrarily stipulated that if $p(A)=0$ then both $p(A \Rightarrow B)$ and $p(A \Rightarrow -B)$ equal 1, from which it would follow that the contrary $A \Rightarrow -B$ could not be a 'true' denial of $A \Rightarrow B$ since in fact the two would be probabilistically consistent. Lacking a satisfactory theory of the zero antecedent probability case, all that can be argued is that results which hold true of conditionals when their antecedents don't have probability zero constitute *prima facie* evidence for their validity in general, although we must always be prepared to find that our supposed generalities admit exceptions in the zero antecedent case. The same holds true with regard to findings about probabilistic soundness, for instance that the Narrowed Hypothetical Syllogism schema is universally sound. At best we will be able to demonstrate that when the antecedents of "if A then B" and "if A and B then C" have non-zero probabilities and both conditionals are highly probable, then "if A then C" must be highly probable, and the question of what holds when a conditional antecedent has zero probability must be left open. What these remarks suggest is the desirability of serious investigation of the zero-antecedent case, pending which all conclusions concerning it must be regarded as tentative.

NOTES

1 Note the explicit *temporal* aspect of the situation described, where one 'premise' was known prior to the second's being learned. Temporal aspects of reasoning will not be considered in Chapters I–III, but will be taken up in Chapter IV, especially in IV.9 and IV.10.

2 Entropic uncertainty (see, e.g. Khinchin [35]) will be only occasionally relevant to the concerns of this book (for instance as it can be used to describe the effects of information-acquisition and its 'inverse', probability mixing, as in Section 2), and this type of uncertainty is obviously very different from probability of falsity. In fact, maximum probability of falsity entails minimum entropic uncertainty.

3 Brian Ellis [17] and [18] has also independently developed a probabilistic theory of the logic of conditionals which in many respects parallels the present theory. A fundamental difference between Ellis' approach and the present one is that he treats probability as a 'concept of truth'. Limitations of space preclude a detailed comparison with the present theory.

4 Probably the most radical implication of the present approach is that we are no longer able to give a uniform 'semantics' for arbitrary iterations of compounding by conditionalization, or of forming other sentential compounds with conditional constituents (see Section 8, where these matters are discussed in some detail). Lewis [40] has taken this implication in particular as showing that the present approach makes *too* radical a departure from orthodox theory.

5 We will attempt so far as possible in this work to sidestep problems having to do with defining $p(A \Rightarrow B)$ when $p(A)$ equals 0. In earlier papers [1] and [2] I made a conventional stipulation that $p(A \Rightarrow B) = 1$ when $p(A) = 0$, but here we have preferred to leave the 'zero antecedent probability case' an open problem, and have tried to indicate to what extent we may expect further developments in the probabilistic logic of conditionals to depend on that special case.

6 The argument of this paragraph can be made entirely rigorous so far as it applies to the theory formulated in [1] and [2], where $p(A \Rightarrow B)$ is defined to be 1 when $p(A)$ is 0. In this case $p(A \Rightarrow B)$ is *always* a function of $p(A)$ and $p(A \& B)$, and the argument shows that this would entail that $t(A \Rightarrow B)$ should be a function of $t(A)$ and $t(A \& B)$. In this case a 'triviality argument' paralleling the one immediately following would

show that for any A and probability function p, either $p(A)=0$ or $p(A)=1$: i.e., the only possible probability values would be truth values.

[7] There is an exception in the case of the self-contradictory $(A \& -A)$, or more generally any combination $A \& B$ where A and B are represented as disjoint. These are of course propositions with probability 0.

[8] Zoltan Domotor in private conversation has suggested dealing with the zero antecedent probability problem by representing probabilities in a non-Archimedean ordered vector space (which would allow some probabilities to be 'incomparably small' with respect to others). The details of this intriguing suggestion remain to be worked out.

[9] We will be able to make only incidental remarks in this work about 'conditional related' connectives like 'even if', 'only if', and 'unless'. The most natural reading of 'A, even if B' is as a *conjunction*, "A, and if B then A". Thus, 'even if' includes 'if', but is much stronger. On the truth-conditional analysis, "A, even if B" comes out equivalent to A, but this depends on the material conditional fallacy that A entails "if B then A". Note that our probabilistic 'semantics' does not allow us to attach a probability to even-if constructions, since these are conjunctions with conditional conjuncts, which we will show in Section 8 to involve difficulties for probability.

[10] Ones first reaction to this example is that it is a special instance of the fallacy of material implication to infer $-A \Rightarrow B$ from A. That is, one is apt to interpret a speaker who makes an assertion of the form "if it is the case that if A then B, then B" as saying no more than A. However, there are reasons for thinking the compound in question is more nearly equivalent to $A \vee B$, in which case the fallacy is more complicated.

[11] The intuitive inconsistency of the conditionals $A \Rightarrow B$ and $A \Rightarrow -B$ is assumed in Lewis Carroll's intriguing 'barbershop paradox' [14] (not to be confused with the 'paradox' of the barber who shaves all men in town who don't shave themselves). Assuming our probabilistic interpretation of conditionals, the paradox is not resolved by pointing out that $A \Rightarrow B$ and $A \Rightarrow -B$ are *not* inconsistent, for probabilistically they are inconsistent. However, other features of Carroll's paradoxical argument, and in particular its being of the *Reductio ad Absurdum* form involving *counterfactuals*, put it beyond the reach of the present analysis.

CHAPTER II

MATHEMATICAL THEORY OF PROBABILISTIC CONSISTENCY AND UNIVERSAL PROBABILISTIC SOUNDNESS

1. INTRODUCTION

This chapter will be primarily concerned with the question: it is possible for the premises of an inference schema to be highly probable at the same time that its conclusion is improbable, and more generally, how low a conclusion probability is compatible with given high premise probabilities for inferences of that pattern? This is the problem of determining universal probabilistic soundness, but as noted in Section I.8 it proves most convenient to approach this problem *via* a consideration of *probabilistic consistency*. In what follows we will give mathematical precizations of the concepts of universal probabilistic soundness and probabilistic consistency which have so far been used in a rough informal way, and then derive some general results concerning them. As we will be mainly concerned with mathematical theory in what follows, basic methodological issues will be left aside for the present. A few preliminary foundational remarks are in order, however.

How is the concept of a *possible probability* to be made precise? We will sidestep this difficult question and simply postulate that any description of probabilities which is consistent with standard axioms of probability (principally the so-called Kolmogorov Axioms [36]) describes possible probabilities. Without getting involved in the probably futile effort to justify this postulate, we must at least note that in making it we import into our theory certain idealizations and difficulties. For now we will ignore the fact that probabilities *change* as a result of acquiring factual information. That is, when we ask whether it is possible for premises to be probable and conclusions improbable we will be trying to find out whether these probabilities can exist at a single instant of time, and not whether it is possible for the premises to be highly probable at one time and for the conclusion to be improbable at another. This might seem to be a reasonable restriction, but we will see in Chapter IV that certain kinds of deductive phenomena cannot be properly understood unless the fact that new premises represent new information (which may reflect back on previously arrived at conclusions) is taken into account. In particular, certain patterns of inference with two or more premises like *Modus Tollens* which 'look perfectly sound' when probability change is ignored prove to have exceptions when it is taken account of.

A second idealization in standard theory is implicit in its assumption that when a factual proposition is probable then any of its logical consequences must be at least as probable. In effect, it is being assumed that persons ought to be instantly aware of the logical consequences of whatever factual propositions they believe. This idealization is unfortunate in applications of probability which are designed to throw light on processes of deductive reasoning, but there simply doesn't exist a theory which takes into account 'logical myopia' and which is applicable to the questions which concern us.[1] Therefore we are stuck for now with the idealization, and we must keep in mind that when and if theoreies are evolved which avoid the idealization, some of our present results may be brought into question.

Also, we must mention again the problem of conditionals whose antecedents have probability 0. We sidestep the problem of dealing with them by banishing from our language all conditionals whose antecedents necessarily have zero probability (logically false antecedents) and by excluding from consideration possible probability functions which assign zero probability to the antecedent of any conditional involved, when we seek to determine the universal probabilistic soundness of a particular inference schema. In effect, what we determine is not *absolute* probabilistic soundness, but rather probabilistic soundness *relative* the particular soundness test we employ (which avoids considering probability functions attaching zero probabilities to the antecedents of conditionals). Thus relative probabilistic soundness becomes a necessary but not necessarily a sufficient condition for absolute (universal) probabilistic soundness.

How are 'highly probable' and 'probable' to be interpreted in the probablistic soundness requirement that the fact that the premises of an inference are highly probable should guarantee that the conclusion is probable? Rather than attempt a direct precization we reformulate the requirement in what seems at first sight an arbitrary manner into a *certifiability of the conclusion* requirement roughly to the effect that it should be possible to assure an arbitrarily high degree of certitude in the conclusion (short of perfect certainty) by making sufficiently sure of the premises (short of requiring perfect certainty in them). This is made precise in Section 4, but the point to be made here is that the interest in the certifiability criterion is not so much in certifiability for its own sake, but in properties which can be shown to be directly related to it. We are able to show, for instance, that if inferences fail to satisfy the certifiability requirement then it is not possible to assure *any* degree of certainty in their conclusions, no matter how certain the premises are required to be. Also we are able to give precise bounds on the degree of possible uncertainty in a 'certifiable conclusion' as a function of the uncertainties of the premises. In effect, then, the vague idea of probabilistic soundness gets replaced by a more precise one, and this in turn is of interest primarily because it serves as a convenient tool for the study of a variety of questions relating to probabilistic aspects of deductive reasoning involving conditionals.

2. PRELIMINARY DEFINITIONS

The first concepts to be defined are syntactical ones, leading to the characterization of formal languages for expressing conditionals. We will work with *sentential variables*, which will be capital letters '*A*', '*B*', etc., possibly with numeral subscripts, plus the two sentential constants '*T*' and '*F*' which are to be informally regarded as expressing a logical truth and a logical falsehood, respectively. Any set of sentential variables together with '*T*' and '*F*' generates a *factual language*, which is the set of all expressions which can be formed from these symbols either alone or by arbitrary iterations of the unary connective '−' (negation), or the binary connectives '&' (conjunction), '∨' (disjunction), or '⊃' (the material conditional). A factual language is a *sublanguage* of another (and the second is an extension of the first) if all formulas of the first are also formulas of the second; a language is *finite* if it has a finite number of atomic formulas. The notions of logical consistency and logical consequence will be assumed to apply to formulas and sets of formulas of a factual language in the usual way, with the proviso that '*T*' is logically true and '*F*' is logically false. We will normally not explicitly specify the factual language of concern, except in the particular case where it is essential that it be finite. Lower case Greek letters will be used as variables ranging over factual formulas (formulas of a factual language).

Given a factual language $\mathscr{L}$, its *conditional extension* is defined to be the set of all formulas of $\mathscr{L}$ together with all expressions of the form $\phi \Rightarrow \psi$, where ϕ and ψ are formulas of $\mathscr{L}$ and ϕ is not logically false. The latter will be called *conditional formulas* of $\mathscr{L}$ (and the terms 'antecedent' and 'consequent' will be applied in the usual way), the conditional extension will be called a *conditional language*, and $\mathscr{L}$ will be called its *factual basis*. Note that the connective '$\Rightarrow$' can occur only as the main connective in a formula (in contrast to the standard sentential connectives), corresponding to the fact that probabilities are not defined for compounds with conditional constituents. The exclusion of conditionals with logically false antecedents arises because it would be impossible to assign non-zero probability to such conditionals. Script capitals '$\mathscr{A}$', '$\mathscr{B}$', etc., will be used as variables ranging over both factual and conditional formulas of a conditional language, and capital letters 'X', 'Y', etc., will be used as variables ranging over *sets* of these formulas.

The following are some further bits of syntactical terminology. Given a factual formula ϕ, its *conditionalization* is defined to be the formula $T \Rightarrow \phi$. Factual formulas are 'probabilistically equivalent' to their conditionalizations in a sense to be defined shortly. The *material counterpart* of the conditional formula $\phi \Rightarrow \psi$ is defined to be the factual formula $\phi \supset \psi$; it results from replacing the double barred arrow by the material implication symbol. We will take the material counterpart of a factual formula to be the formula itself. The material counterpart of a conditional with non-logically true antecedent is never probabilistically equivalent to it. The *contrary* of a factual formula is defined to be its negation, while the contrary of the conditional $\phi \Rightarrow \psi$ is defined as before to be the conditional $\phi \Rightarrow -\psi$. If $\mathscr{A}$ is either factual or conditional we will use '$\sim \mathscr{A}$' as the metalinguistic abbreviation for the contrary of $\mathscr{A}$. For any set X of such formulas, $\sim X$ will be taken to be the set of contraries of formulas of X.

Now let X be the finite non-empty set of conditional formulas $\{\phi_1 \Rightarrow \psi_1, \ldots, \phi_n \Rightarrow \psi_n\}$. The *quasi-conjunction* of the formulas of X is defined to be the conditional formula

$$C(X) = (\phi_1 \vee \ldots \vee \phi_n) \Rightarrow [(\phi_1 \supset \psi_1) \& \ldots \& (\phi_n \supset \psi_n)].$$

The quasi-conjunction operation is extended to sets X containing factual formulas by the device of substituting for each factual formula involved its conditionalization. This operation is easily seen to be commutative, associative and idempotent up to probabilistic equivalence, and to reduce to ordinary conjunction in the special case in which all of the formulas conjoined are factual. In the general case quasi-conjunction is not a 'true' conjunction operation since, though every finite set of formulas entails its quasi-conjunction (in a sense of 'entails' still to be defined), the quasi-conjunction does not entail all formulas of the set. The dual operation of *quasi-disjunction* is defined for finite sets X of conditional formulas to be

$$D(X) = (\phi_1 \vee ,,, \vee \phi_n) \Rightarrow [(\phi_1 \,\&\, \psi_1) \vee \dots \vee (\phi_n \,\&\, \psi_n)].$$

Again the operation is extended to sets including factual formulas by substituting the conditionalizations for each factual formula involved. Quasi-disjunction reduces to ordinary disjunction in application to factual formulas, but is not a 'true' disjunction since the quasi-disjunction of a set of formulas is not in general entailed (in a sense still to be defined) by all formulas of the set.

The next series of definitions concerns what might be called the 'truth-conditional semantics' of factual and conditional languages. Given a factual language, $\mathscr{L}$, a *truth-assignment* for $\mathscr{L}$ is a function, t, mapping the formulas of $\mathscr{L}$ into the numbers 0 (for 'falsity') and 1 (for 'truth') such that $t(T)=1$ and $t(F)=0$ (note the henceforth we shall use formulas like 'T' and 'F' autonomously), and satisfying the usual laws of sentential combination (in particular, $t(\phi \supset \psi)$ is 1 if and only if either $t(\phi)=0$ or $t(\psi)=1$, so that '$\supset$' is interpreted as the material conditional). If the language is finite, there are only a finite number of distinct truth-assignments for it, and each such assignment, t, can be made to correspond to a *state-description*, ϕ_t, which is a formula of the language, and such that for any factual formula ϕ of $\mathscr{L}$, $E(\phi)=1$ if and only if ϕ is logically consistent with ϕ_t.

Now consider a factual language $\mathscr{L}$, a truth-assignment t for $\mathscr{L}$, and a conditional formula $\phi \Rightarrow \psi$ in the conditional extension of $\mathscr{L}$. We will say that $\phi \Rightarrow \psi$ is *verified* under t if $t(\phi)=t(\psi)=1$, and $\phi \Rightarrow \psi$ is *falsified* under t if $t(\phi)=1$ and $t(\psi)=0$. $\phi \Rightarrow \psi$ is neither verified nor falsified under t if $t(\phi)=0$. The notions of verification and falsification are extended to factual formulas by identifying them with their conditionalizations. With this convention, a factual formula ϕ is verified or falsified under t according as $t(\phi)$ is 1 or 0. Observe that while conditional formulas may be neither verified nor falsified under a truth-assignment, factual formulas must have one of the two 'verification values'.

Some important properties of verification and falsification are as follows. By definition, the conditionalization of a factual formula is verified or falsified under a truth-assignment according as the formula itself is. Given a conditional formula $\phi \Rightarrow \psi$, its material counterpart is falsified under t if and only if it is falsified under t, while the material counterpart is verified under t if and only if the conditional is not falsified (though it may not be verified either). The contrary of a formula is verified if and only if the formula is falsified, and is falsified if and only if the formula is verified. The quasi-conjunction $C(X)$ of a finite set of formulas is verified under t if and only if no member of X is falsified and *at least one is verified* under t. $C(X)$ is falsified under t if and only if at least one member of X is falsified under t. The only case in which $C(X)$ is neither verified nor falsified under t is that in which no member of X is verified and no member of X is falsified under t. The quasi-disjunction $D(X)$ is verified under t if and only if at least one member of X is verified under t, and $D(X)$ is falsified under t if and only if no member of X is verified and at least one member is falsified under t. The special cases in which $C(X)$ is verified and in which $D(X)$ is falsified are important. In the former we shall say that the set X itself is *confirmed* by t (no member is falsified and at least one is verified), and in the latter we shall say that X is *disconfirmed* by t (no member is verified and at least one is falsified). X is *confirmable* if there exists a truth-assignment confirming it, and is *disconfirmable* if there exists a truth-assignment disconfirming it.

Some obvious interconnections among the foregoing notions are the following. t verifies or falsifies $\sim(\sim \mathscr{A})$ according as it verifies $\mathscr{A}$ ($\mathscr{A}$ and $\sim(\sim \mathscr{A})$ are 'verification equivalent'). Similarly, $C(\sim X)$ is verification equivalent to $\sim D(X)$ and $D(\sim X)$ is verification equivalent to $\sim C(X)$. t confirms X if and only if it disconfirms $\sim X$, and disconfirms X if and only if it confirms $\sim X$.

The final series of preliminary definitions has to do with probability. Given a factual language $\mathscr{L}$, a *probability-assignment* for $\mathscr{L}$ is a function p mapping the formulas of $\mathscr{L}$ into real numbers in the interval from 0 to 1 (inclusive) in such a way as to satisfy the *Kolmogorov Axioms*: (1) if ϕ

logically entails ψ then $p(\phi) \leqslant p(\psi)$, and $p(T)=1$, and (2) if ϕ and ψ are logically inconsistent then $p(\phi \vee \psi) = p(\phi) + p(\psi)$. These axioms ential the familiar laws of probability, as they are developed in the first chapter of any elementary probability text, and these laws will be taken for granted here.

Some particular facts to be noted about probability functions are the following. The first is that truth-assignments for a factual language are *ipso facto* probability-assignments for the language, and in fact a probability-assignment is a truth assignment if and only if it assigns solely the 'extreme values' 0 and 1 to formulas of the language. Second, if the language is finite so that each truth-assignment t is associated with a formula ϕ_t of the language in the way previously described (any formula ϕ is consistent with ϕ_t if and only if $t(\phi)=1$), then the probability $p(t)$ can be identified with $p(\phi_t)$, and for any formula ϕ,

$$(1) \qquad p(\phi) = p(t_1)\, t_1(\phi) + \cdots + p(t_n)\, t_n(\phi),$$

where $t_1, \ldots, t_n$ are all of the truth-assignments for the language. Equation (1) can be interpreted as saying that the probability of any proposition ϕ is equal to the sum of the probabilities of the states of affairs (truth-assignments) t_i in which it would be true (i.e., in which $t_i(\phi)=1$). Finally, if p is a probability function for any factual language $\mathscr{L}$, and $\mathscr{L}$ is a sub-language of another factual language $\mathscr{L}'$, then there is a probability function p' for $\mathscr{L}'$ such that $p'(\phi)=p(\phi)$ for all ϕ in $\mathscr{L}$.

Given a probability function p for a factual language $\mathscr{L}$, and a formula ϕ of $\mathscr{L}$, the *uncertainty* of ϕ relative to p is the number $u_p(\phi)=p(-\phi)= 1 - p(\phi)$. The uncertainty of ϕ measures the degree to which ϕ is regarded as unlikely. Two easily demonstrable facts about uncertainty as here characterized are that if ϕ entails ψ then $u_p(\psi)$ is no greater than $u_p(\phi)$, and that $u_p(\phi_1 \& \ldots \& \phi_n)$ is no greater than the sum of the uncertainties $u_p(\phi_i)$ for $i=1, \ldots, n$. Combined, the foregoing imply that if a factual formula is a logical consequence of a finite set of such formulas, then the uncertainty of the consequence is no greater than the sum of the un-certainties of the premises. A generalization of this will be seen to hold in the case of conditionals, which we consider next.

Given a factual language $\mathscr{L}$, a probability-assignment for it, p, and a conditional formula $\phi \Rightarrow \psi$ of its conditional extension, p will be said to be *proper* for $\phi \Rightarrow \psi$ if $p(\phi)$ is not 0. If X is a set of factual and/or conditional formulas of the conditional extension, then p is *proper* for X if it is proper for all conditional formulas of X. It is seldom the case that truth-assignments, considered as probability-assignments, are proper for sets X including conditionals, but it is trivial that if X is finite there exist proper probability-assignments for X (this depends critically on the fact that conditional formulas with logically false antecedents are excluded).

Now let $\mathscr{L}$ be a factual language, p be a probability-assignment for $\mathscr{L}$, and let $\phi \Rightarrow \psi$ be a conditional formula of the conditional extension of $\mathscr{L}$ such that p is proper for $\phi \Rightarrow \psi$. The *conditional probability* of $\phi \Rightarrow \psi$ *relative to* p is then defined to be the ratio $p(\phi \ \& \ \psi)/p(\phi)$. The *uncertainty* of $\phi \Rightarrow \psi$ relative to p is defined as before to be $1 - p(\phi \Rightarrow \psi)$. Various properties of conditional probability and uncertainty which we will have occasion to use include the following. Suppose ϕ is a factual formula of $\mathscr{L}$, $\mathscr{A}$ is a conditional formula of its conditional extension, and X is a finite set of factual and/or conditional formulas such that p is proper for $\mathscr{A}$ and X. (1) $p(\phi) = P(T \Rightarrow \phi)$. (2) if ϕ is the material counterpart of $\mathscr{A}$ then $p(\mathscr{A}) \leqslant p(\phi)$. (3) $p(\sim \mathscr{A}) = 1 - p(\mathscr{A})$. (4) $p(\sim D(X)) = p(C(\sim X))$ and $p(\sim C(X)) = p(D(\sim X))$. (5) $p(D(X))$ is no greater the sum of the probabilities $p(\mathscr{B})$ for $\mathscr{B}$ in X. (6) $u_p(C(X))$ is no greater than the sum of the uncertainties $u_p(\mathscr{B})$ for $\mathscr{B}$ in X. Conditions (1) and (4) entail that ϕ and $T \Rightarrow \phi$, $\sim D(X)$ and $C(\sim X)$, and $\sim C(X)$ and $D(\sim X)$ are *probabilistically equivalent* in the sense that each member of any of the pairs must be equal in probability to the other member of the pair, relative to any probability-assignment. We have already noted that these pairs are also verification-equivalent in the sense that one member of the pair must be verified or falsified according as the other is by any truth-assignment, and this is a special case of the general rule that if two formulas are verification-equivalent they are also probabilistically equivalent.

The general rule just stated follows immediately from the following generalization of Equation (1). If $\mathscr{L}$ is finite, p is a probability-assignment for $\mathscr{L}$, and p is proper for the conditional formula $\phi \Rightarrow \psi$ of the conditional extension of $\mathscr{L}$, then

$$(2) \qquad p(\phi \Rightarrow \psi) = \frac{p(t_1) \, t_1(\phi \ \& \ \psi) + \cdots + p(t_n) \, t_n(\phi \ \& \ \psi)}{p(t_1) \, t_1(\phi) + \cdots + p(t_n) \, t_n(\phi)}$$

where $t_1, ..., t_n$ are the truth-assignments for $\mathscr{L}$. Informally interpreted, equation (2) says that the probability of a conditional $\phi \Rightarrow \psi$ is equal to the probability of its being verified (in which case $t_i(\phi \ \& \ \psi) = 1$) divided by the probability of its being either verified or falsified (this being the case where $t_i(\phi)=1$). This is a generalization of the 'probability equals probability of truth' equation which reduces to the latter in case the formula involved is factual, since in the latter case the formula has probability 1 of being either verified or falsified. It will be seen that this generalization is not only technically useful, but appears to have a significance for the *meaning* of conditional probability, which will emerge in Chapter III.

3. PROBABILISTIC CONSISTENCY

The following definition provides a precise if somewhat arbitrary characterization of the informal idea of probabilistic consistency discussed in Section I.9.

DEFINITION 1. Let $\mathcal{L}$ be a factual language and let X be a set of formulas of its conditional extension. X is *probabilistically-consistent* (abbr. 'p-consistent') if and only if for all real numbers $\varepsilon > 0$, there exist probability-assignments p for $\mathcal{L}$ which are proper for X such that $p(\mathcal{A}) \geqslant 1-\varepsilon$ for all $\mathcal{A}$ in X.

In words, a set of formulas is probabilistically consistent if it is possible for all formulas of the set to be as close to certain as desired, short of being perfectly certain. We might have imposed a still stronger requirement for a set X to be probabilistically consistent: namely that there be some probability-assignment such that $p(\mathcal{A})=1$ for all $\mathcal{A}$ in X, hence that all members of X be absolutely certain. This requirement would be intuitively too strong, however, since imposing it would mean that the two formulas 'A' and '$B \Rightarrow -A$' (example: 'the sun will rise tomorrow' and 'if the universe ends today the sun will not rise tomorrow') would not be probabilistically consistent in this sense. The requirement that it should be possible for all members of a probabilistically consistent set to be arbitrarily close to complete certainty might in fact seem too strong itself. However we will see in a moment that where a set does not satisfy this requirement there are fixed upper limits as to how probable all of its members can be.

An important fact to note about the definition of p-consistency is that it does not satisfy the *compactness condition*, and therefore we cannot expect the concept of probabilistic soundness which is in a sense 'based on it' to satisfy all of the usual laws for deduction relations. An example of an infinite set of formulas which is p-inconsistent, though no finite subset of it is p-inconsistent, is the following: the set of all formulas '$(A_i \lor A_{i+1}) \Rightarrow (A_{i+1} \,\&\, -A_i)$' where '$A_1$', '$A_2$', ...are atomic formulas of an infinite language. It will follow from Theorem 1.2 below that any finite subset of the above set is p-consistent, but it is easily seen that if each formula of the above set had probability at least $1-\varepsilon$, then for each i, $p(A_i)$ would be no greater than $\varepsilon/(1-\varepsilon)$ times $p(A_{i+1})$, which would entail that $p(A_1)$ would have to be zero if there were an infinite number of atomic formulas. But this would mean that the probability function p would not be proper for the set of all of these formulas.

The foregoing example is illustrative of the fact that our imposition of the requirement that the probability-assignments to be dealt with must be *proper* has some unexpected and non-trivial implications where we consider infinite sets of formulas and their probabilistic consistency. For this reason we will henceforth restrict ourselves to considering just finite sets of formulas and inferences with only finite numbers of premises.

Theorem 1 below gives necessary and sufficient conditions for finite sets of formulas to be probabilistically consistent, and in fact provides us with a decision procedure for determining probabilistic consistency for such sets.

THEOREM 1. Let $\mathscr{L}$ be a factual language, let p be a probability-assignment for $\mathscr{L}$, and let X be a finite set of formulas of the conditional extension of $\mathscr{L}$ such that p is proper for X.

1.1.   If there exists a non-empty subset of X which is not confirmable, then the sum of the uncertainties $u_p(\mathscr{A})$ for $\mathscr{A}$ in X is at least 1, and hence X is not p-consistent.

1.2.   If every non-empty subset of X is confirmable then X is p-consistent.

Proof of 1.1. Suppose that some non-empty subset Y of X is not confirmable. We have seen (Section 2) that this is equivalent to supposing that the quasi-conjunction $C(Y)$ is not verifiable, and this entails by Equation (2) that $p(C(Y))=0$, hence $u_p(C(Y))=1$. It is also the case that the uncertainty of a quasi-conjunction is less than or equal to the sum of the uncertainties of its quasi-conjuncts, hence the sum of the uncertainties $u_p(\mathscr{A})$ for $\mathscr{A}$ in Y is at least 1. *A fortiori* the sum for $\mathscr{A}$ in X is at least 1.

Proof of 1.2. Suppose that every non-empty subset Y of X is confirmable: i.e., there exists a truth-assignment t_Y for $\mathscr{L}$ which does not falsify any formula of Y, and verifies at least one. It is possible to construct a finite 'nested decreasing sequence' of non-empty subsets of X, namely $X_1, ..., X_n$ (where $X_1 = X$), and associated sequence of truth-assignments $t_{X_1}, ..., t_{X_n}$ confirming $X_1, ..., X_n$, respectively, such that: (1) X_{i+1} is the proper subset of X_i consisting of all formulas of the latter *not* verified by t_{X_i}, for $i = 1, ..., n-1$, and (2) t_{X_n} verifies all formulas of X_n. That X_{i+1} is always a *proper* subset of X_i depends on the fact that t_{X_i} confirms X_i, hence verifies at least one member of it. This series of subsets X_i and confirming truth-assignments t_{X_i} is easily seen to satisfy the further conditions that: (1) every $\mathscr{A}$ in X either belongs to X_n or to a unique Y_i defined to be the set of all $\mathscr{B}$ in X_i which are not in X_{i+1}, for $i = 1, ..., n-1$, (2) t_i verifies all formulas in Y_i and neither verifies nor falsifies any formulas in $Y_1, ..., Y_{i-1}$, for $i = 1, ..., n-1$, and (3) t_{X_n} verifies all formulas in X_n and neither verifies nor falsifies any formula of $Y_1, ... Y_{n-1}$.

Now, as we can assume without loss of generality that we are dealing with a finite language, we can use Equation (1) to define a probability-assignment for the language by assigning probability values to its possible truth-assignments. We do this in the following way. For $i = 1, ..., n-1$, we define

$$p(t_{X_i}) = \varepsilon^{i-1}(1 - \varepsilon),$$

and set

$$p(t_{X_n}) = \varepsilon^{n-1}.$$

For any truth-assignment not among the t_{X_i}, we set its probability equal to 0. It follows immediately from Equation (1), then, that for any factual formula ϕ of the language,

$$p(\phi) = p(t_{X_1})t_{X_1}(\phi) + \cdots + p(t_{X_n})t_{X_n}(\phi).$$

It must now be shown that, given the foregoing definition of the probability-assignment p, $p(\mathscr{A}) \geqslant 1 - \varepsilon$ for all $\mathscr{A}$ in X. We can assume without loss of generality that $\mathscr{A}$ is conditional, say $\mathscr{A} = \phi \Rightarrow \psi$, since otherwise $\mathscr{A}$ can be replaced by its conditionalization. It follows from Equation (2) then that

$$p(\mathscr{A}) = \frac{p(t_{X_1})\,t_{X_1}(\phi\,\&\,\psi) + \cdots + p(t_{X_n})\,t_{X_n}(\phi\,\&\,\psi)}{p(t_{X_1})\,t_{X_1}(\phi) + \cdots + p(t_{X_n})\,t_{X_n}(\phi)}.$$

$\mathscr{A}$ must belong to a unique Y_i or to X_n, and this means that $t_{X_j}(\phi)=t_{X_j}(\phi\ \&\ \psi)=0$ for $j=1,...,i-1$, while $t_{X_i}(\phi)=t_{Xi}(\phi\ \&\ \psi)=1$ (since t_{X_i} verifies all formulas of Y_i, or verifies all formulas of X_i if $i=n$). It follows that all terms in the sums in the numerator and denominator of the above ratio for $j=1,...,i-1$ are 0, while $p(t_{X_i})t_{Xi}(\phi\ \&\ \psi)=p(t_{X_i})t_{X_i}(\phi)=p(t_{X_i})$, and the latter equals $\varepsilon^{i-1}(1-\varepsilon)$ if $i<n$, or ε^{n-1} if $i=n$. The latter trivially implies that

$$p(\mathscr{A}) \geqslant \frac{\varepsilon^{i-1}(1-\varepsilon)}{\varepsilon^{i-1}(1-\varepsilon)+\varepsilon^i(1-\varepsilon)+\cdots+\varepsilon^{n-1}} = 1-\varepsilon,$$

if $i<n$, and

$$p(\mathscr{A}) = 1$$

if $i=n$. In either case, therefore, $p(\mathscr{A})\geqslant 1-\varepsilon$, hence all members of X can be assigned probabilities arbitrarily close to 1, and the theorem is proved.

Theorem 1 simultaneously provides a decision procedure for determining probabilistic consistency and tells us how high the probabilities of formulas in probabilistically inconsistent sets can be. To determine whether a set has a non-empty subset which is not confirmable can be done mechanically since this is a matter of finding out whether there exists a truth-assignment not falsifying any member of the subset and verifying at least one. Three examples of probabilistically inconsistent sets are: (1) the set whose only member is '$A \Rightarrow -A$', (2) the set whose members are '$A \Rightarrow B$' and '$A \Rightarrow -B$', and (3) the three-member set containing the formulas '$A \Rightarrow B$', '$(A\ \&\ B) \Rightarrow C$' and '$A \Rightarrow -C$'. It is obvious in the first case that no truth-assignment can confirm '$A \Rightarrow -A$', since this would require that both 'A' and '$-A$' be verified. Similarly the two-member set containing '$A \Rightarrow B$' and '$A \Rightarrow -B$' could not be confirmed since any truth-assignment verifying one member would have to make 'A' true, hence would falsify the other member.

Theorem 1.1 tells us that in each of the probabilistically inconsistent sets above, the sum of the uncertainties of the formulas of the set (relative to any proper probability assignment) must be at least 1. This means that in the first case, the uncertainty $u_p(A \Rightarrow -A)$ must equal 1, hence the probability $p(A \Rightarrow -A)$ must equal 0. In the second case the two uncertainties $u_p(A \Rightarrow B)$ and $u_p(A \Rightarrow -B)$ cannot be simultaneously greater than 1/2. In general, given an n-member p-inconsistent set of formulas, the fact that their uncertainties must total at least 1 means that not all members of the set can have probabilities greater than $1-1/n$. Note that if n is large, however, the probabilities of all members of a probabilistically inconsistent set *can* be quite high, though not 'arbitrarily high'.

Examples of sets which are probabilistically consistent, since all non-empty subsets of them are confirmable, are: (1) the two-member set containing '$A \vee B$' and '$A \Rightarrow -B$', and (2) the three-member set containing '$A \Rightarrow B$', '$B \Rightarrow C$' and '$A \Rightarrow -C$'. In the first case, for instance, the truth-assignment t such that $t(A)=0$ and $t(B)=1$ confirms the whole set since it verifies '$A \vee B$' and neither verifies nor falsifies '$A \Rightarrow -B$'. The same truth-assignment confirms the one member subset containing '$A \vee B$', and the truth-assignment t' such that $t'(A)=1$ and $t'(B)=0$ confirms the one-member subset containing '$A \Rightarrow -B$'. In the case of set (2), the truth-assignment t such that $t(A)=0$ while $t(B)=t(C)=1$ confirms the entire set, and it is easy to find truth-assignments confirming the non-empty proper subsets.

The following theorem lists some further properties of probabilistic consistency which have intuitive significance. No proofs will be given since the parts of the theorem follow almost trivially from basic definitions plus Theorem 1.

THEOREM 2. Let $\mathscr{A}$ be a factual or conditional formula, let X be a finite set of such formulas, and let X' be the set of material counterparts of formulas in X.

2.1.   If X' is logically inconsistent than X is probabilistically inconsistent.

2.2.   If X is probabilistically inconsistent and contains at least one factual formula and no proper subset of X is probabilistically inconsistent, then X' is logically inconsistent.

2.3.   If X is probabilistically consistent then either $X \cup \{\mathscr{A}\}$ $X \cup \{\sim\mathscr{A}\}$ is probabilistically consistent.

Part 2.1 tells us that the logical inconsistency of the material counterparts is sufficient for the originals to be probabilistically inconsistent. For instance, the three formulas 'A', '$A \Rightarrow B$' and '$-B$' have logically inconsistent material counterparts, hence they are probabilistically inconsistent (by Theorem 1.1 they cannot all have probabilities in excess of 2/3). Logical inconsistency is not necessary for probabilistic inconsistency since we already know that the two formulas '$A \Rightarrow B$' and '$A \Rightarrow -B$' are probabilistically inconsistent, though their material counterparts are obviously logically consistent.

Part 2.2 gives an important special case in which logical inconsistency (of the material counterparts) is necessary for a set X to be probabilistically consistent. This is that in which X contains a factual formula and none of its proper subsets is probabilistically inconsistent. An example is the two-member set containing '$A \lor B$' and '$A \Rightarrow -B$', whose first member is factual, and were it is obvious that no proper subset of the set is probabilistically inconsistent. Knowing that the material counterparts of the formulas of the set are logically consistent then insures that the set itself is probabilistically consistent. Part 2.2 is illustrative of a striking difference between the probabilistic logic of sets of purely conditional formulas and that of sets of mixed conditional and factual formulas. In the purely conditional case, as we have seen, 'truth conditional inconsistency' (i.e., truth-conditional inconsistency of the material counterparts) is sufficient but not necessary for probabilistic consistency. In the case of mixed sets, if the subset of purely conditional formulas is probabilistically consistent, then the entire set is probabilistically consistent if and only if it is 'truth-conditionally' so. We will see related differences between the logic of mixed as against pure sets of conditional propositions brought out in Theorems 3.4 and 3.7, which concern probabilistic entailment.

Part 2.3 is cited here to illustrate the fact that the operation of forming the contrary stands to probabilistic inconsistency much as ordinary negation stands to truth-conditional inconsistency.

4. PROBABILISTIC ENTAILMENT

As already noted, we choose not to give a direct precization of the intuitive probabilistic soundness requirement, but rather to consider a formalization of the *certifiability of the conclusion* requirement that it must be possible to assure an arbitrarily high degree of certitude in the conclusion of an inference by making sufficiently sure of the premises. This requirement is formulated in Definition 2 below:

DEFINITION 2. Let $\mathscr{L}$ be a factual language, let $\mathscr{A}$ be a formula of its conditional extension, and let X be a set of such formulas. Then X *probabilistically entails* $\mathscr{A}$ (abbr. 'X *p-entails* $\mathscr{A}$') if for all $\varepsilon > 0$ there exists $\delta > 0$ such that for all probability-assignments p for $\mathscr{L}$ which are proper for X and $\mathscr{A}$, if $p(\mathscr{B}) \geqslant 1 - \delta$ for all $\mathscr{B}$ in X, then $p(\mathscr{A}) \geqslant 1 - \varepsilon$.

The use of the term 'entailment' applying to the probabilistic-entailment relation just defined must be justified by showing that this relation satisfies at least some of the laws which entailment or deduction relations are ordinarily assumed to satisfy (see, e.g., Henkin and Montague [30]). As a matter of fact this relation does not satisfy all of these laws, since it does not satisfy the compactness principal (our earlier example of an infinite set which is p-inconsistent though no finite subset is one in which the infinite set p-entails 'F' while no finite subset does). It can be shown that p-entailment does satisfy the two most essential laws for deduction relations among finite sets of premises, and in fact any conclusion p-entailed by a finite set of premises can be derived from them within a natural deduction format using rather simple rules of inference. Before turning to questions of deducibility, though, we list some elementary properties of the p-entailment relation, and in particular ones which implicitly provide us with a decision procedure for determining when a conclusion is p-entailed by a finite set of premises. No proofs will be given for the parts of the following theorem, since each part is an easy consequence of basic definitions plus previous theorems.

THEOREM 3. Let $\mathscr{L}$ be a factual language, let $\mathscr{A}$ and $\mathscr{B}$ be formulas of its conditional extension, and let X be a finite set of such formulas. Let p be a probability-assignment for $\mathscr{L}$ which is proper for $\mathscr{A}$, $\mathscr{B}$ and X. Let $\mathscr{A}'$ be the material counterpart of $\mathscr{A}$ and let X' be the set of all material counterparts of formulas in X.

3.1.   If X p-entails $\mathscr{A}$ then $u_p(\mathscr{A})$ is no greater than the sum of the uncertainties $u_p(\mathscr{B})$ for $\mathscr{B}$ in X.

3.2.   If X does not p-entail $\mathscr{A}$ then for all $\varepsilon > 0$ there exists a probability-assignment q for $\mathscr{L}$ which is proper for $\mathscr{A}$ and X such that $q(\mathscr{B}) \geqslant 1 - \varepsilon$ for all $\mathscr{B}$ in X, but $q(\mathscr{A}) \leqslant \varepsilon$.

3.3.   If X is p-consistent and p-entails $\mathscr{A}$ then X' logically entails $\mathscr{A}'$.

3.4.   If X' logically entails $\mathscr{A}'$ and $\mathscr{A}$ is factual, then X p-entails $\mathscr{A}$.

3.5. X p-entails $\mathscr{A}$ if and only if $X \cup \{ \sim\mathscr{A} \}$ is p-inconsistent; X p-entails all formulas if and only if it is p-inconsistent.

3.6.   If $X \cup \{ \mathscr{B} \}$ and $X \cup \{ \sim\mathscr{B} \}$ both p-entail $\mathscr{A}$ then X p-entails $\mathscr{A}$.

3.7.   If $\mathscr{A}$ is conditional, X contains at least one factual formula, and X p-entails $\mathscr{A}$ but no proper subset of X p-entails $\mathscr{A}$, then X p-entails both the antecedent and consequent of $\mathscr{A}$.

3.8.   If 'A' is a sentential variable not occurring in X and ϕ is a factual formula, then X p-entails $A \Rightarrow \phi$ if and only if either X is p-inconsistent or $A \supset \phi$ is logically true.

A few comments may help to bring out the significance of the different parts of Theorem 3. 3.1 generalizes the rule stated in Section I.1 that if a factual formula is a logical consequence of a finite set of factual formulas then the uncertainty of the conclusion is no greater than the sum of the uncertainties of the premises. Note that in going over to conditionals, though, we speak of p-entailment rather than logical consequence. 3.2 shows that where a conclusion is not p-entailed, arbitrarily high probabilities for the premises are compatible with arbitrarily low probabilities for the conclusion.

3.3 and 3.4 are intended to bring out connections between p-entailment relations among conditionals and logical consequence relations among their material counterparts. Where we are dealing with p-consistent premises, then the fact that the conclusion (more exactly, its material counterpart) is logically implied is at least a necessary condition for it to be p-entailed. That logical entailment is not sufficient for p-entailment is obvious, since the factual formula $A \supset B$ logically entails the material counterpart of $A \Rightarrow B$ (which is $A \supset B$), but does not p-entail $A \Rightarrow B$ itself. Where the conclusion is itself factual, however, then 3.4 says that being a logical consequence of premises is also a sufficient condition for a conclusion to be p-entailed by them. Thus, where rules of inference which are sound truth-conditionally lead from conditional or unconditional premises to factual conclusions (as do *Modus Ponens* and *Modus Tollens*) their truth-conditional soundness does assure their probabilistic soundness.[2]

Part 3.5 is most important, since it yields an immediate decision procedure for determining whether a conclusion $\mathscr{A}$ is p-entailed by a finite set of premises, X: namely by determining whether the set of X together with the contrary of $\mathscr{A}$ is p-consistent. For example, to determine whether the factual formula $A \supset B$ p-entails the conditional $A \Rightarrow B$, it is necessary to determine whether the two formulas $A \supset B$ and $A \Rightarrow -B$ are p-consistent. The truth-assignment t such that $t(A) = t(B) = 0$ verifies the first formula and neither verifies nor falsifies the second, hence the entire set is confirmable, hence the set is p-consistent and so $A \supset B$ does not p-entail $A \Rightarrow B$. An example of an inference which is p-sound (the premises p-entail the conclusion) is to infer $A \Rightarrow C$ from the premises $A \Rightarrow B$ and $(A \& B) \Rightarrow C$ (this is the Narrowed Hypothetical Syllogism introduced in Section I.5). This is shown to be p-sound since the set containing the three formulas $A \Rightarrow B$, $(A \& B) \Rightarrow C$ and $A \Rightarrow -C$ is not confirmable.

Parts 3.5 and 3.6 together show that p-entailment satisfies certain laws of 'indirect inference' (reasoning from assumptions which are ultimately 'discharged' in the course of the reasoning) which are analogous to familiar principals of indirect truth-conditional inference. 3.5, for instance, is a kind of generalization of *reductio ad absurdum* inference, since it says that a conclusion is p-entailed if the contrary would be inconsistent (i.e., p-inconsistent) with given premises. 3.6 is a generalization of the 'proof by cases' pattern of indirect reasoning. Not all rules of indirect truth-conditional reasoning generalize neatly to probabilistic counterparts, the familiar conditionalization rule being an example: i.e., that if ψ follows from X plus an assumption ϕ then $\phi \Rightarrow \psi$ follows from X alone. Indeed, if this rule were valid, then as we have seen the conditional $A \Rightarrow B$ could be derived from the material conditional, and the ordinary conditional could be represented as a material conditional for the purposes of determining the soundness of arguments involving it.

Part 3.7 is like part 2 of Theorem 2 in bringing out a striking difference between the logic of purely conditional propositions and that of mixed conditional and factual propositions. What 3.7 says in effect is that if a conditional conclusion is p-entailed by premises including factual propositions, and the inference *depends* on its factual premises (the conclusion doesn't follow if the factual premises are removed), then in fact not only does the conditional follow, but its antecedent and consequent as well. An illustration is the inference of $A \Rightarrow B$ from the two premises A and B, which is easily seen to be p-sound, but where in fact it would be very odd to deduce the conditional since the much stronger that conclusion both the antecedent and consequent can be asserted follows. Thus, it would appear that in the normal case in which conditionals are inferred, if the inference is probabilistically sound at all, it cannot depend on factual premises. This raises interesting logical questions as to just what does justify reasoning which issues in conditional conclusions, assuming it must ultimately be grounded in factual 'data', but these are matters which cannot be pursued further here.

Part 3.8 is cited here to show that probabilistic considerations lend some support to the vague but not uncommon intuition that one should not be able to infer a conditional proposition about what would happen *if* a state of affairs, A, arose, from premises which do not 'refer' to that state of affairs. Students are apt to suggest that this is what is wrong in the 'fallacy' of material implication, to infer 'if A then B' from B, as in the example 'Jones will win; therefore, if it rained yesterday, Jones will win'. Now we see that if these inferences are symbolizable in such a way that the antecedent of the concluding conditional is represented by a sentential variable not occurring among the premises, they can only be probabilistically sound if either the premises are p-inconsistent (where they p-entail anything), or the conclusion is logically true (so that anything p-entails it).

The final series of theorems primarily concern deducibility relations among conditionals. Part 4.2, asserting that p-entailed conclusions can always be deduced following certain rules of inference, is not as precisely stated as might be, since we have not spelled out precisely what it means to say that a conclusion within our language is derivable by given rules from premises. This notion can be defined in the usual way, however, and we shall simply take it for granted here.

THEOREM 4. Let $\mathscr{L}$ be a factual language, let ϕ, ψ, and η be formulas of $\mathscr{L}$, let $\mathscr{A}$ be a formula of the conditional extension of $\mathscr{L}$, and let X and Y be finite sets of such formulas.

4.1. X p-entails all of its members, and if X p-entails all members of Y and Y p-entails $\mathscr{A}$, then X p-entails $\mathscr{A}$.

4.2. X p-entails $\mathscr{A}$ if and only if $\mathscr{A}$ is derivable from X using the following seven rules of inference:
R1. $T \Rightarrow \phi$ and ϕ are interderivable.

R2. If ϕ is logically consistent and ϕ and ψ are logically equivalent then $\phi \Rightarrow \eta$ can be derived from $\psi \Rightarrow \eta$.

R3. If ϕ is logically consistent and logically entails ψ, then $\phi \Rightarrow \psi$ can be derived from the empty set.

R4. $(\phi \lor \psi) \Rightarrow \eta$ can be derived from $\phi \Rightarrow \eta$ and $\psi \Rightarrow \eta$.

R5. If $\phi \,\&\, \psi$ is logically consistent then $(\phi \,\&\, \psi) \Rightarrow \eta$ can be derived from $\phi \Rightarrow \eta$ and $\phi \Rightarrow \psi$.

R6. $\phi \Rightarrow \eta$ can be derived from $\phi \Rightarrow \psi$ and $(\phi \,\&\, \psi) \Rightarrow \eta$.

R7. If ϕ is logically consistent but $\phi \,\&\, \psi$ is logically inconsistent, then anything can be derived from $\phi \Rightarrow \psi$.

4.3. Assume that $A_1, ..., A_n$ and B are distinct sentential variables of $\mathscr{L}$. There is no set X of formulas of the conditional extension of $\mathscr{L}$ with less than n members which is p-equivalent to the set

$$\{A_1 \Rightarrow B, ..., A_n \Rightarrow B\}$$

in the sense that all members of X are p-entailed by this set and X p-entails all members of this set.

Proof of 4.1. That X p-entails all of its own members is trivial. To prove that if X p-entails all members of Y and Y p-entails $\mathscr{A}$, then X p-entails $\mathscr{A}$, we introduce the following notion of *yielding*. A set Z *yields* $\mathscr{A}$ if: (1) every truth-assignment confirming Z verifies $\mathscr{A}$, and (2) every truth-assignment falsifying $\mathscr{A}$ falsifies at least one member of Z. It is easy to show that a set Z p-entails $\mathscr{A}$ if and only if either Z is p-inconsistent or some subset of Z (possibly empty) yields $\mathscr{A}$. The only case in which $\mathscr{A}$ is yielded by an empty set is that in which $\mathscr{A}$ is a 'p-tautology'; i.e., no truth-assignment falsifies $\mathscr{A}$.

Now suppose that X p-entails all members of Y and Y p-entails $\mathscr{A}$. If X is p-inconsistent, obviously X p-entails $\mathscr{A}$. Suppose X is not p-inconsistent. Then for every $\mathscr{B}$ in Y there is a subset $X_{\mathscr{B}}$ of X which yields $\mathscr{B}$. It will be shown first that Y must itself be p-consistent, since every non-empty subset of it, Z, must be confirmable. Let X_Z be the union of the sets $X_{\mathscr{B}}$ for $\mathscr{B}$ in Z. If X_Z is empty, this can only arise if all members of Z are p-tautologies, hence it is trivial that Z is confirmable. If X_Z is non-empty then it is confirmable; say truth-assignment t confirms X_Z. It is easy to see in this case that t confirms Z itself, and hence Z is confirmable. Therefore every non-empty subset of Y is confirmable, hence Y is p-consistent.

If Y is p-consistent and p-entails $\mathscr{A}$, then there is a subset Z of Y yielding $\mathscr{A}$. If Z is empty, $\mathscr{A}$ is a p-tautology, and trivially X p-entails $\mathscr{A}$. If Z is non-empty, form the subset X_Z as the union of all subsets $X_{\mathscr{B}}$ yielding members $\mathscr{B}$ of Z. It is easy to show that X_Z itself must yield $\mathscr{A}$, and therefore X p-entails $\mathscr{A}$ since it has a subset which yields $\mathscr{A}$.

Proof of 4.2. That conclusions derivable from premises by R1–R7 are p-entailed by them follows immediately from the facts that: (1) immediate inferences in accord with these rules lead from premises to p-entailed conclusions, and (2) that p-entailed consequences of formulas which are p-entailed by premises are p-entailed by the premises. The latter has been established in 4.1, and the former is easily verified by showing that each of R1–R7 leads from premises to conclusions such that the set consisting of the premises together with the contrary of the conclusion is not confirmable, which is sufficient for the premises to p-entail the conclusion by Theorems 1.1 and 3.5.

To show that if $\mathscr{A}$ is p-entailed by a finite set X, then $\mathscr{A}$ is derivable from X by iterated applications of R1–R7, suppose that $\mathscr{A}$ is p-entailed by X. We can suppose that X is 'minimal' in the sense that no proper subset of X p-entails $\mathscr{A}$. If X is empty then it is trivial that it can only p-entail $\mathscr{A}$ if the material counterpart of $\mathscr{A}$ is logically true, in which case $\mathscr{A}$ follows from the empty set by R3.

Suppose now that X is not empty. It is an easy consequence of earlier theorems that, since X is minimal and X p-entails $\mathscr{A}$, the quasi-conjunction $C(X)$ also p-entails $\mathscr{A}$. We will show, proving a series of 'derived inference rules' such that anything derivable by them must be derivable by R1–R7, that $C(X)$ is derivable from X by those rules, and $\mathscr{A}$ is derivable from $C(X)$ by them. The derived rules are set out below, together with outlines of the steps by which inferences in accord with the derived rules can be reduced to ones in accord either with the basic ones or previous derived rules. Only in the reduction of R8, the first derived rule, will the steps be outlined in detail.

> R8. If ϕ logically implies ψ then $\eta \Rightarrow \psi$ can be derived from $\eta \Rightarrow \phi$

Reduction. Suppose ϕ logically implies ψ. Assume first that $\eta \,\&\, \phi$ is logically consistent. The derivation of $\eta \Rightarrow \psi$ from $\eta \Rightarrow \phi$ in this case goes as follows. (Step 1) $\eta \Rightarrow \phi$ (given). (Step 2) $(\eta \,\&\, \phi) \Rightarrow \psi$ (from the empty set by R3, since $\eta \,\&\, \phi$ logically implies ψ). (Step 3) $\eta \Rightarrow \psi$ (from Steps 1 and 2, by R6).

Now assume that $\eta \,\&\, \phi$ is not logically consistent. In this case the derivation of $\eta \Rightarrow \psi$ from $\eta \Rightarrow \phi$ goes as follows. (Step 1) $\eta \Rightarrow \phi$ (given). (Step 2) $\eta \Rightarrow \psi$ (from Step 1 by R7, since $\eta \,\&\, \phi$ is logically inconsistent).

R9. $\phi \Rightarrow (\psi \,\&\, \eta)$ can be derived from $\phi \Rightarrow \psi$ and $\phi \Rightarrow \eta$.

Reduction. Case 1: $\phi \,\&\, \psi \,\&\, \eta$ is logically consistent. (1) $\phi \Rightarrow \psi$ (given). (2) $\phi \Rightarrow \eta$ (given). (3) $(\phi \,\&\, \psi) \Rightarrow \eta$ (steps 1, 2, R5). (4) $(\phi \,\&\, \psi) \,\&\, \eta \Rightarrow \psi \,\&\, \eta$ (R3). (5) $\phi \,\&\, \psi \Rightarrow \psi \,\&\, \eta$ (3, 4, R6). (6) $\phi \Rightarrow \psi \,\&\, \eta$ (1, 5, R6).

Case 2: $\phi \,\&\, \psi$ is consistent but $\phi \,\&\, \psi \,\&\, \eta$ is inconsistent. (1) $\phi \Rightarrow \psi$ (given). (2) $\phi \Rightarrow \eta$ (given). (3) $(\phi \,\&\, \psi) \Rightarrow \eta$ (1, 2, R5). (4) $\phi \Rightarrow (\psi \,\&\, \eta)$ (3, R7, using fact that $\phi \,\&\, \psi \,\&\, \eta$ is inconsistent).

Case 3: $\phi \,\&\, \psi$ is inconsistent. (1) $\phi \Rightarrow \psi$ (given). (2) $\phi \Rightarrow (\psi \,\&\, \eta)$ (1, R7, using fact that $\phi \,\&\, \psi$ is inconsistent).

R10. $\phi \Rightarrow \psi$ can be derived from $\phi \Rightarrow (\psi \,\&\, \eta)$.

Reduction. Case 1: $\phi \,\&\, \psi \,\&\, \eta$ is consistent. (1) $\phi \Rightarrow \psi \,\&\, \eta$ (given). (2) $\phi \,\&\, (\psi \,\&\, \eta) \Rightarrow \psi$ (from empty set, by R3). (3) $\phi \Rightarrow \psi$ (1, 2, R6).

Case 2: $\phi \,\&\, \psi \,\&\, \eta$ is inconsistent. (1) $\phi \Rightarrow (\psi \,\&\, \eta)$ (given). (2) $\phi \Rightarrow \psi$ (1, R7).

R11. $(\phi \lor \eta) \Rightarrow (\phi \supset \psi)$ can be derived from $\phi \Rightarrow \psi$.

Reduction. Case 1: both $\phi \,\&\, \psi$ and $\eta \,\&\, -\phi$ are consistent. (1) $\phi \Rightarrow \psi$ (given). (2) $(\phi \,\&\, \psi) \Rightarrow (\phi \supset \psi)$ (from empty set, by R3). (3) $\phi \Rightarrow (\phi \supset \psi)$ (1, 2, R6). (4) $(\eta \,\&\, -\phi) \Rightarrow (\phi \supset \psi)$ (from empty set, by R3). (5) $(\phi \lor (\eta \,\&\, \& -\phi)) \Rightarrow (\phi \supset \psi)$ (3, 4, R4). (6) $(\phi \lor \eta) \Rightarrow (\phi \supset \psi)$ (5, R2).

Case 2: $\phi \,\&\, \psi$ is consistent but $\eta \,\&\, -\phi$ is inconsistent. (1) $\phi \Rightarrow \psi$ (given). (2) $(\phi \,\&\, \psi) \Rightarrow (\phi \supset \psi)$ (R3). (3) $\phi \Rightarrow (\phi \supset \psi)$ (1, 2, R6). (4) $(\phi \lor \eta) \Rightarrow (\phi \supset \psi)$ (3, R2, since $\phi \lor \eta$ is logically equivalent to ϕ). Case 3: $\phi \,\&\, \psi$ is inconsistent. (1) $\phi \Rightarrow \psi$ (given). (2) $(\phi \lor \eta) \Rightarrow (\phi \supset \psi)$ (1, R7).

R12. $(\phi_1 \lor \phi_2) \Rightarrow ((\phi_1 \supset \psi_1) \,\&\, (\phi_2 \supset \psi_2))$ is derivable from $\phi_1 \Rightarrow \psi_1$ and $\phi_2 \Rightarrow \psi_2$.

Reduction. (1) $\phi_1 \Rightarrow \psi_1$ (given). (2) $\phi_2 \Rightarrow \psi_2$ (given). (3) $(\phi_1 \lor \phi_2) \Rightarrow$

$\Rightarrow (\phi_1 \supset \phi_1)$ (1, R11). (4) $(\phi_2 \vee \phi_1) \Rightarrow (\phi_2 \supset \psi_2)$ (2, R11). (5) $(\phi_1 \vee \phi_2) \Rightarrow$
$\Rightarrow (\phi_2 \supset \psi_2)$ (4, R2). (6) $(\phi_1 \vee \phi_2) \Rightarrow ((\phi_1 \supset \psi_1) \,\&\, (\phi_2 \supset \psi_2))$ (3, 5, R9).

R13. C(S) can be derived from S.

Reduction. Case 1: All formulas of S are conditional. R13 then follows
by iterated applications of R12.

Case 2: Some formulas of S are factual. The conditionalizations of
these formulas can be derived from them by R1, and the case is there-
after reduced to Case 1.

R14. If $\phi_1 \,\&\, \psi_1$ logically implies $\phi_2 \,\&\, \psi_2$ and $\phi_1 \supset \psi_1$ logically implies $\phi_2 \supset \psi_2$ then $\phi_2 \Rightarrow \psi_2$ can be derived from
$\phi_1 \Rightarrow \psi_1$.

Reduction. Case 1: both $\phi_1 \,\&\, \psi_1 \,\&\, \phi_2$ and $\phi_2 \,\&\, -\phi_1$ are consistent.
(1) $\phi_1 \Rightarrow \psi_1$ (given). (2) $\phi_1 \,\&\, \psi_1 \Rightarrow \phi_2 \,\&\, \psi_2$ (R3). (3) $\phi_1 \Rightarrow \phi_2 \,\&\, \psi_2$ (1, 2,
R6). (4) $\phi_1 \Rightarrow \phi_2$ (3, R10). (5) $\phi_1 \Rightarrow \psi_2 \,\&\, \phi_2$ (3, R8). (6) $\phi_1 \Rightarrow \psi_2$ (5, R10).
(7) $\phi_1 \,\&\, \phi_2 \Rightarrow \psi_2$ (4, 6, R5). (8) $-\phi_1 \,\&\, \phi_2 \Rightarrow \psi_2$ (R3, using fact that
$\phi_1 \supset \psi_1$ logically implies $\phi_2 \supset \psi_2$). (9) $((\phi_1 \,\&\, \phi_2) \vee (-\phi_1 \,\&\, \phi_2)) \Rightarrow \psi_2$
(7, 8, R4). (10) $\phi_2 \Rightarrow \psi_2$ (9, R2).

Case 2: $\phi_1 \,\&\, \psi_1 \,\&\, \phi_2$ is inconsistent, but $\phi_2 \,\&\, -\phi_1$ is inconsistent.
Steps 1–7 same as Case 1. (8) $\phi_2 \Rightarrow \phi_1$ (R3, using fact that $\phi_2 \,\&\, -\phi_1$ is
inconsistent). (9) $\phi_2 \Rightarrow \psi_2$ (8, 7, R6).

Case 3: $\phi_1 \,\&\, \psi_1 \,\&\, \phi_2$ is inconsistent, but $\phi_1 \,\&\, \psi_1$ is consistent. (1)
$\phi_1 \,\&\, \psi_1 \Rightarrow \phi_2 \,\&\, \psi_2$ (R3, using fact that $\phi_1 \,\&\, \psi_1$ logically implies $\phi_2 \,\&\, \psi_2$).
(2) $\phi_2 \Rightarrow \psi_2$ (1, R7, using fact that $\phi_1 \,\&\, \psi_1 \,\&\, \phi_2 \,\&\, \psi_2$ is logically inconsistent).

Case 4: $\phi_1 \,\&\, \psi_1$ is inconsistent. (1) $\phi_1 \Rightarrow \psi_1$ (given). (2) $\phi_2 \Rightarrow \psi_2$ (1, R7).

R15. If $\mathscr{A}$ and $\mathscr{B}$ are factual or conditional and $\mathscr{A}$ p-entails
$\mathscr{B}$ then $\mathscr{B}$ can be derived from $\mathscr{A}$.

Reduction. Case 1: $\mathscr{B}$ is p-entailed by the empty set, and is conditional:
say $\mathscr{B} = \phi \Rightarrow \psi$. Then ϕ must logically imply ψ, hence $\phi \Rightarrow \psi$ can be derived
from the empty set by R3.

Case 2. $\mathscr{B}$ is p-entailed by the empty set, and is factual, say $\mathscr{B} = \phi$. Then
clearly ϕ is logically true, hence is logically implied by T. $T \Rightarrow \phi$ is derivable from the empty set oy R3, and ϕ is derivable from $T \Rightarrow \phi$ by R1.

Case 3. $\mathscr{B}$ is not p-entailed by the empty set, both $\mathscr{A}$ and $\mathscr{B}$ are conditional, say $\mathscr{A} = \phi_1 \Rightarrow \psi_1$ and $\mathscr{B} = \phi_2 \Rightarrow \psi_2$. It must be the case that $\phi_1 \& \psi_1$ logically implies $\phi_2 \& \psi_2$, and $\phi_1 \supset \psi_1$ implies $\phi_2 \supset \psi_2$ (this is what is required for $\mathscr{A}$ to 'yield' $\mathscr{B}$). By R14, $\mathscr{B}$ is derivable from $\mathscr{A}$ in this case.

Case 4. $\mathscr{B}$ is not p-entailed by the empty set, one or both of $\mathscr{A}$ or $\mathscr{B}$ is factual. This case is reduced to Case 3 by deriving the material counterparts of the factual formulas involved from them, and conversely, according to R1.

This concludes the proof of 4.2.

Proof of 4.3. Let X be the set of conditionals $\{A_1 \Rightarrow B, ..., A_n \Rightarrow B\}$; it must be shown that there is no set Y of $n-1$ or less members p-equivalent to X in the sense that all members of Y are p-entailed by X and all members of X are p-entailed by Y. Suppose Y were such a set. It can be supposed without loss of generality that no member of Y is p-entailed by the empty set, for otherwise that member could be deleted from Y and the remaining members of Y would also be p-equivalent to X. For every member $\mathscr{A}$ of Y, there must be a subset $X_{\mathscr{A}}$ of X such that $C(X_{\mathscr{A}})$ p-entails $\mathscr{A}$. The set Z of all the quasi-conjunctions $C(X_{\mathscr{A}})$ for $\mathscr{A}$ in Y must also be p-equivalent to X, for quasi-conjunctions of members of a set are p-entailed by the set, and since all members of Y are p-entailed by these quasi-conjunctions, and all members of X are p-entailed by Y, all members of X are p-entailed by Z. Z is therefore a set of less than n members, all of whose members are quasi-conjunctions of members of X, and which is p-equivalent to X. It is easy to show, however, that a set of quasi-conjunctions of members of X can only p-entail a member of X if in fact that member of X is included in the set of quasi-conjunctions entailing it. Hence Z would have to actually contain all members of X, and so have at least n members, contrary to assumption.

We conclude with some informal remarks on the significance of the results given in Theorem 4. Part 4.1 of course substantiates what we have all along assumed: i.e., that p-entailment at least satisfies those entailment-theoretic conditions which are essential if it is even to make sense to characterize this relation in terms of derivability in accord with rules of inference. Part 4.2 shows p-entailment to be so characterizable, in terms of a rather small set of simple rules. The extent to which this characterization throws light on real life reasoning involving conditionals may perhaps be doubted (perhaps real life reasoning is best understood in terms of inferences in accord with partially sound rules), but at least there is some intrinsic interest to the rules themselves which makes them worthy of independent comment.

Observe that rule R1 (that the conditionalization, $T \Rightarrow \phi$, of a factual formula ϕ can be deduced from it, and conversely) is the only one of the seven rules linking factual and conditional propositions, and this link is trivial. In fact it is easily demonstrated that in deducing conditional conclusions from conditional premises it is never necessary to use R1: the path from conditional to conditional need never proceed by way of the factual. Our rules have the peculiarity that in going from factual to factual formulas it is necessary to go by way of conditionals, as is obviously necessitated by the fact that all of the usual rules of sentential logic are here packed into conditional rules like R3.

Rule R2, that logically equivalent propositions are intersubstitutable in the antecedents of conditionals, requires no special comment beyond reiterating the point made in Chapter 1, Section 6 that there are apparent violations of this principle in the case of conditionals with disjunctive antecedents. Accepting the validity of the principle therefore requires us to regard conditionals whose antecedents are grammatical disjunctions (and possibly ones whose antecedents are grammatical negations of conjunctions) as being of a different logical form to be symbolized accordingly (as conjunctions of conditionals).

R3 permits the derivation of a *conditional tautology* (a conditional whose antecedent logically implies its consequent) from anything. It is intuitively plausible that conditionals of this sort should be affirmable 'no matter what'.

R4 involves the tricky conditional with disjunctive antecedent. Regarding the ordinary language "if either A or B then C" as equivalent to the joint assertion of "if A then C" and "if B then C", what R4 says in effect is that the *logical* $(A \lor B) \Rightarrow C$ can be derived from "if either A or B then C". The converse, however, is not universally probabilistically sound, since this is essentially the disjunctive narrowing rule discussed in Section I.6.

R5 can be looked on as specifying special circumstances under which the *conjunctive narrowing* pattern, to infer $(A \& B) \Rightarrow C$ from $A \Rightarrow C$, is sound (we noted in Section I.3 that it is not universally sound). This is the case in which not only $A \Rightarrow C$ can be affirmed but $A \Rightarrow B$ as well. Thus, we can narrow the antecedent A in the conditional "if A then C" by adding to A anything probabilistically implied by A. Of course, this is not the only situation in which conjunctive narrowing is sound, but this is all that needs to be assumed in order to be able to deduce all universally sound consequences.

R6 is of course the Narrowed Hypothetical Syllogism which has been discussed at length in Section I.5. Note that it is here formulated in such a way as to be a kind of converse to the special conjunctive narrowing schema of R5. If we regard $A \Rightarrow B$ as antecedently given, then R5 says that $(A \text{ & } B) \Rightarrow C$ can be derived from $A \Rightarrow C$, and R6 says that $A \Rightarrow C$ can be derived from $(A \text{ & } B) \Rightarrow C$. Combined, R5 and R6 assert that given $A \Rightarrow B$, the propositions $A \Rightarrow C$ and $(A \text{ & } B) \Rightarrow C$ are equivalent.

The import of R7 is that anything can be derived from p-inconsistent premises. This shares the doubtfulness of any claims about the consequences of inconsistent premises, which we are forced into by virtue of our basing the definition of probabilistic soundness on a possible worlds semantics (albeit a possible *probabilistic* worlds semantics), and which will be returned to in Section IV.9. The rule has the added drawback that it is the one most critically dependent on arbitrary aspects of our formulation, and in particular on our exclusion of conditionals with inconsistent antecedents and exclusion of improper probability functions. In fact, in an earlier formulation (Adams [1] and [2]) inconsistent antecedents and improper probability functions were allowed (with the arbitrary stipulation that $P(A=B)=1$ if $P(A)=0$), and it can be shown that the valid rules for the earlier formulation are interderivable with our present rules R1–R6 (but now interpreted so as to apply to conditionals with inconsistent antecedents). Thus, R1–R6 appear to be relatively 'robust' in that they do not seem to depend on arbitrary aspects of the formalism, while R7 can be regarded as the syntactic expression of our exclusion of improper probability functions from the semantics. In any case, R7 should not be regarded as implying anything about what it would actually be rational to infer from inconsistent 'data'. It is probably significant in this connection that R7 is the only one of our rules which is not also valid when the conditionals involved are treated as material conditionals.

Theorem 4.3 shows that our formal language does not include any single formula $\phi \Rightarrow \psi$ which acts like the *conjunction* of the two formulas

$A_1 \Rightarrow B$ and $A_2 \Rightarrow B$ relative to the p-entailment relation: i.e., no formula $\phi \Rightarrow \psi$ is both p-entailed by $A_1 \Rightarrow B$ and $A_2 \Rightarrow B$ and p-entails these two formulas. More generally, any set

$$\{A_1 \Rightarrow B, ..., A_n \Rightarrow B\}$$

cannot be reduced to a smaller p-equivalent set, so there is no limit to the size of the p-irreducible premise sets which we may have to consider. Of course, it is trivial that our formal language can be *extended* by adding 'formal conjunctions' to it which act like conjunctions relative to the p-entailment relation. As we have already seen, however, the price which must be paid for making such an extension is that our probabilistic semantics cannot be extended to it in a 'natural' way (Lewis' triviality result).

NOTES

[1] Except, see Hintikka (32).

[2] This basic theorem has been given in Suppes [46] and Adams [2], and is apparently widely known to probability theorists. Adams and Levine [7] state a partial converse to it which holds when all of the propositions involved in an inference are factual, and all premises are essential: namely that the maximum possible uncertainty of the conclusion *equals* the sum of the uncertainties of the premises, or else 1, whichever is least. Adams and Levine also apply linear programming analysis to determine maximum conclusion uncertainties where there are various kinds of redundancies among the premises (e.g., where $(A \& B) \vee (A \& C) \vee (B \& C)$ is inferred from A, B, and C). Interesting unsolved problems remain in determining maximum conclusion uncertainties in inferences involving conditionals. The following is a striking fact which suggests that such an investigation might have intriguing results. The minimum probability of the conclusion, B, of the 'direct' *Modus Ponens* inference with premises A and $A \Rightarrow B$ equals the product of the probabilities of the premises, while the maximum uncertainty of the conclusion $-A$ of the 'inverse' *Modus Tollens* inference with premises $A \Rightarrow B$ and $-B$ equals the uncertainty of $-B$ *divided* by the probability of $A \Rightarrow B$. In the direct case minimum conclusion probability is directly proportional to the conditional premise's probability, and in the inverse case the maximum conclusion uncertainty is inversely proportional to the conditional premise's probability.

[3] We must reiterate here that this holds only in cases where all premises, either of the *Modus Ponens* inference or of the *Modus Tollens* inference, are probable *at the same time*. We will see in 1V.1 that when the conditional $A \Rightarrow B$ is accepted at one time and then $-B$ is learned, it is not always rational to infer $-A$. This is connected with the fact that where the premise of a *Modus Tollens* inference is *counterfactual*, of the form "if A were the case then B would be", it may not be rational to affirm $-A$ even though $-B$ is accepted at the same time (though this is controversial – see Section IV.4).

CHAPTER III

MOTIVES FOR WANTING TO ASSURE THE SOUNDNESS OF REASONING; TRUTH AND PROBABILITY AS DESIRABLE ATTRIBUTES OF CONCLUSIONS REACHED IN REASONING

1. INTRODUCTION: AIMS AND METHODS

This chapter is ultimately concerned with the basic assumptions of the theory of probabilistic soundness developed in Chapters 1 and 2, and in particular with the legitimacy of the ratio representation of the probabilities of conditionals, and with the 'probability equals probability of truth' assumptions which entail that truth-conditional soundness guarantees probabilistic soundness in the case of inferences involving only factual propositions. These issues will not be approached in the way which is usual in current literature on 'foundational questions' concerning truth and probability: namely as matters of *conceptual analysis*, where one might hope, for example, to show by analysis of the concept of probability that the probabilities of conditionals are 'appropriately measured' as ratios. We shall begin instead by considering what 'attributes' of conclusions, which are perhaps only crudely described by the words 'truth' and 'probability', persons might have motives for wanting in the conclusions they arrive at in their reasoning, which might in turn motivate their efforts to assure the soundness of this reasoning. We shall indeed find reasons why persons should want to arrive at conclusions which are 'true' in a kind of 'correspondence' sense under certain circumstances, and why they should under similar circumstances want to arrive at conditional conclusions only when their *ratio* probabilities are high, and these will be regarded as supporting the basic assumptions of our theory by at least showing why persons should *want* to assure the kind of soundness which our probabilistic soundness tests are capable of showing. It is a further question, which we shall not enter into here, whether this sense of 'true' and the ratio measure of conditional probabilities are in some way 'part of the meanings of *truth* and *probability*'.

As the foregoing remarks have already suggested, we shall assume that the primary reason people have for wanting to assure the soundness of their reasoning arises from their desire to reach 'the right' conclusions by

it. Thus, to more clearly understand motives for trying to assure soundness, we must understand why people should under certain circumstances
want their conclusions to be of the right kinds. In trying to come to grips
with this question, we shall consider one kind of motive only: namely a
pragmatic motive arising from the fact that people often *act* on their
conclusions, and it is plausible to suppose that the results of their actions,
good or bad, may depend on the rightness of the conclusions acted on.
This leads us to inquire in some detail into how conclusions of different
kinds which can be reached in reasoning may influence behavior, and how
the good or bad results of this behavior may be related to the 'rightness'
of these conclusions. Considering the latter question leads us in turn first
into the currently very active field of the theory of *reason and action*,
and second, when we come to ask how conclusions about *probabilities*
affect behavior, into the domain of theories of *decision making under
risk*.

To anticipate a bit, we shall find one carefully worked out theory of
action (more exactly, a theory of action-descriptions), due to D. S.
Shwayder, which relates four 'factors' of interest to us – belief, truth,
action, and success – in such a way as to suggest a strong reason for
wanting to hold beliefs (which might be the conclusions arrived at in
reasoning) which are true in a kind of *correspondence* sense, assuming
persons to act on them. Turning to the question as to how conclusions
about probabilities influence behavior, the *expected utility theory* of
decisions based on estimated probabilities, which is well known in the
literature of statistics and the behavioral sciences, furnishes an elegant
description of this influence, which also can be turned to account in
explaining why it should be desirable to estimate probabilities *correctly*
if persons making these estimates hope to be 'best off in the long run',
assuming that there are objective limitations on how often it is possible to
be right in conclusions about particular matters of fact. These considerations in turn explain why persons should want to arrive at highly probable
conclusions as to matters of fact, in a sense of probability which can be
equated to probability of truth. Finally, considering how persons act on
conclusions of conditional form of one particularly important kind (i.e.,
a conclusion as to what will happen if a particular action is taken) explains
both by we cannot easily attach truth-values to such propositions in such
a way that persons are best off arriving at ones to which the value 'true' is

attached (and not arriving at ones to which the value 'false' is attached), and why one *is* best off in the long run to estimate their probabilities as ratios and act on those estimates.

A couple of preliminary remarks and a major disclaimer are in order, before turning to details. Our concern with the aims of reasoning, and in particular with that of 'arriving at the truth', should be contrasted with some well known and superficially similar considerations relating to truth advanced by Michael Dummett in his article 'Truth' [16], where he says "It is part of the concept of truth that we aim at making true statements." As the quotation suggests, Dummett uses this claim in drawing certain consequences about the *concept* of truth, which shows that his enterprise is different from ours. Two other points of contrast are also worth noting, however. One has to do with the fact that where we are concerned with truth as a possibly desirable or aimed at attribute in the conclusions people arrive at 'for themselves', Dummett is concerned with it as an attribute people aim to assure in what they tell others – following Grice [24, 25] presumably because that is an attribute of the conclusions they want others to reach. This is not to say that Dummett is wrong in his contention concerning the aims of statement-making, but it should be clear that the way in which Dummett supposes truth to be aimed at, and the reasons for aiming at it, are very different from ours.[1]

A somewhat more general difference between Dummett's approach and the present one is that his attempt to get at the concept of truth *via* the aims of statement-making locates his investigation within the general framework of the theory of Speech Acts, hence of language and communication, while our approach is largely independent of such concerns. Though we shall be concerned with *actions* and their motives, the ones we shall be primarily concerned with will not be linguistic, nor involve any attempt to influence the thought or behavior of others.

Our major disclaimer is that we shall not in any way pretend that the results of the investigation to follow are definitive. We shall consider only a very limited class of propositions which might be arrived at as conclusions in reasoning, and only one kind of mot ve for wanting to be right in such conclusions. No implicit claim is made that other kinds of conclusions and other motives for wanting to be right about them are unimportant. Nevertheless, it seems worthwhile to undertake even a very limited investigation of reasoning in relation to its motives, for only thus is it

possible to substantiate claims as to the adequacy of this or that theory
of soundness in reasoning.

2. A MOTIVE FOR TRYING TO REACH TRUE CONCLUSIONS ABOUT CERTAIN PARTICULAR MATTERS OF FACT

It is intuitively plausible to suppose that where persons are guided in their
actions by their beliefs, they are generally better guided if those beliefs are
true than if they are false. This is the case in the following example. A man
wants to meet a friend of his who is expected to arrive at the local airport
on such and such a day. He telephones the Flight Information Desk on
the morning of this day to ask the expected arrival time and is told that
this is 2 p.m. that afternoon. Acting on this information, he drives to the
airport so as to be in time to meet any plane arriving close to 2 p.m. His
action may be described as being done *for the purpose* of meeting his
friend, *in the belief* that his friend would arrive by plane at 2 p.m.[2] The
purpose may be achieved or may fail to be achieved, and it is evident that
whether or not the belief acted on is correct is closely bound up with the
success or failure of the action. *If the belief is true the action is likely to
succeed, while if the belief is false the action is likely to fail.* To the extent
that the foregoing action is typical and to the extent that the foregoing 'belief-truth-action-success' formula is valid, we have a reason why
persons should want the beliefs on which they act to be true. We also
have a motive for such cognitive actions (belief-influencing actions) as
asking for information or, possibly, checking the soundness of reasoning
which issues in conclusions of the kind which can be acted on. We shall
shortly see that the formula is subject to severe limitations, even as an
explanation of the *pragmatic* reasons for wanting to arrive at 'right' conclusions, but first some comments on it are in order.

The belief-truth-action-success formula is consistent with much current
theory of action, and it can be shown to be implicit in at least one, namely
a theory of *action-descriptions* propounded by D. S. Shwayder in *The
Stratification of Behavior* ([49], see especially Part Two). The relevant
points of Shwayder's analysis can be summarized as follows. Shwayder
takes the *form* of an action-description to be one in which certain manifest
animal behavior is described, and a *purpose* is ascribed to that behavior.

An example might be to describe a dog's action as 'digging for a bone', in which the manifest behavior is the digging, and the purpose is to find a bone. The ascription of purpose serves the function of *explaining* the manifest behavior, and therefore action-descriptions are in Shwayder's phrase 'explanations-cum-descriptions'. The ascription of purpose also means that the action must be conceived of as possibly *succeeding* or *failing*, so that a person would not properly identify the action referred to in the description 'digging for a bone' if he did not know what the *conditions of success* (or failure) would be.

Shwayder also takes the further step, which is essential for present purposes, of supposing that action-descriptions, along with ascribing purposes to behavior, also implicitly impute *beliefs* to the agent, to the effect that *the conditions of success are met*. Of course these beliefs need not have any special connection with language (that would be absurd in the case of the dog), but the imputation of belief is clearly consonant with the view that action-descriptions function to explain behavior. It would not make sense to describe an agent as doing something for a purpose if it were not supposed that the agent believed that the action would accomplish the purpose.[3] Given Shwayder's assumptions, it is evident that the belief-truth-action-success formula follows immediately, at least in application to the beliefs which are for Shwayder the ones which are most properly described as those which are *acted on* directly; namely that the conditions of success are met. If the belief that the conditions of success are met is true, then the action presumably will succeed, while if it is false (or one of the beliefs that *a* condition of success is met is false), the action will presumably not succeed.

It is worthwhile remarking on the sense of 'true' which is appropriate to the belief-truth-action-success formula, which is something like a correspondence one. Going back to the dog, a condition for success for his action of digging for a bone is that there should be a bone underground where he is digging, and this also is what would make his belief that there is a bone (a belief that a condition of success is met) true. The correspondence is therefore between what the dog thinks and what is or is not underground. An important complication, however, is that the correspondence is between what the dog thinks at one time and what becomes manifest (perhaps 'comes to pass' would be better) at a later one. The 'facts' in evidence to the dog at the time he *undertakes* to dig are those which importantly influence his action, while those that are 'brought to light' later are those which determine its success. More generally, at the time when agents have the strongest motive for wanting to assure the rightness of the conclusions on which they expect to act, the facts which determine the rightness of these conclusions are not in evidence. Conversely, when the latter facts come to light it is of no immediate practical concern whether or not they confirm prior beliefs, since it is too late by then to do anything about it. The immediate moral for us is to emphasize the *transitory* character of the pragmatic motive to which we have here drawn attention, for wanting to arrive at true conclusions. We also see that it must be difficult if not impossible to account for any practical interest we may have in the rightness of beliefs about the *past* on the basis of such motives, and we now turn very briefly to this and analogous difficulties which show the need to generalize our account of even the practical motives which people may have for wanting to arrive at true conclusions.

We have already seen what the difficulty is in trying to explain practical concern with the correctness of beliefs about the past along the lines already outlined: it is not the agreement or lack of it between those beliefs and the 'facts' which directly determines the success or lack of it of actions which these beliefs may influence. This is not to say that beliefs about the past don't influence action – they clearly do. For instance, the man hoping to meet his friend at the airport would have been importantly influenced if he had been told by the Flight Information Desk that his friend's plane had already landed. But the influence would be described as 'indirect', and determined by the expectations as to the present and future to which knowledge of the past gives rise. Generalizing, we would expect a pragmatic theory of our interest in propositions concerning the past to have to take into account 'inductive' inferences as to the present and future which are made from these propositions, and this is obviously a very complicated matter.

There are two kinds of beliefs which are sometimes regarded as factual, for which only half of the belief-truth-action-success formula holds, and for which in consequence it is possible to explain why one should want to hold ones which are true, but not why one should want to avoid holding ones which are false. These are beliefs about *measured values,* and beliefs expressible as *generalizations.* Consider the proposition that Jones is six feet and one inch tall. In theory at least, this proposition should be considered as false if Jones is six feet and one and one thousanth of an inch tall. However, there is almost no practical action which one can imagine taking on the basis of the belief that Jones is six feet and one inch tall which would not succeed if Jones were six feet and one and one thousanth of an inch tall. In this case, however, the inapplicability of the belief-truth-action-success formula should perhaps not be taken as an indication of the need to generalize the formula, but rather as a sign that in fact we rarely if ever have a reason for wanting to be exactly right about measured values (where there is a continuum of possible values), and therefore appropriate tests for the soundness of reasoning leading to conclusions concerning them should only be required to show that these conclusions are 'sufficiently accurate' for practical purposes.[4]

Similar remarks apply to actions based on conclusions expressible as generalizations. An example might be to drive to the airport so as to arrive by 2 p.m. on a given day (in order to meet the friend), based on the belief that the only planes ever landing at the airport land at 2 p.m. (perhaps there is but one flight per day). What this illustrates is the fact that typical practical actions based on beliefs expressible as generalizations can also be regarded as being based on beliefs expressible as *instances* of the generalizations. If the generalization is true, the instance is true and the action succeeds, but if the generalization is false the instance may still be true and the action still succeed. Thus, we can explain why we should want to arrive at true conclusions expressible as generalizations, but it is not so obvious how to explain why we should want to avoid arriving at false conclusions of this sort. Though it is more doubtful in the present case than it is in the case of conclusions about measured values, it is plausible to assume that it is usually not very important that generalizations arrived at as conclusions have absolutely no exceptions, and therefore that appropriate tests of the soundness of such reasoning should be designed to guard against arriving at conclusions with 'too many' exceptions.[5]

The final example to be mentioned in this section of a type of proposition, practical concern with which it is difficult to account for on the lines so far advanced, is that of ones characteristically expressed as *denials* of particular propositions. The difficulty with them is that it is hard to find *actions* which are plausibly regarded as being based on acceptance of them. For example, the man hoping to meet his friend at the airport might have learned in some way that his friend's plane was *not* going to arrive at 2 p.m. Coming to believe this might have the effect of *deterring* the man from driving to the airport so as to be on hand by 2 p.m. (supposing he had previously formed the intention of doing so) but refraining from acting is not to perform an act in the 'proper' sense, since it cannot be said to have a purpose or to succeed or fail.

The example just given of the influence on behavior of arriving at a negative conclusion suggests that in focusing solely on *actions* which may be taken, based on conclusions arrived at, we have unduly restricted our consideration of the kinds of practical influences beliefs may have. In particular, arriving at the negative conclusion led the person to 'decide' not to drive to the airport, and though this decision is not an action, it has *consequences*, good and bad, in terms of which it and the beliefs leading to it can be evaluated. It turns out that precisely this kind of influence on behavior is what must be taken into account in order to describe the effect on behavior of arriving at conclusions about *probabilities*. Though we are not primarily concerned here with the development of tests for the soundness or reasoning which leads to such conclusions – the application of which might be motivated by practical concerns as to the results of acting on these conclusions – considering the relation between judgments about probability and decision and action may plausibly be supposed to throw light on what 'right' probabilities are, and why these might be connectable to probabilities of truth in the case of factual propositions but not in the case of conditionals. We begin by describing in some detail the well known theory of decision on the basis of *expected utilities*, which characterizes the connection between probability judgments and decisions, and in the succeeding section we consider motives which people might have for wanting to be 'right' in their estimates of probabilities, given that they decide and act on these estimates in accord with the assumptions of the expected utility theory.

3. ACTING ON ESTIMATED PROBABILITIES; THE EXPECTED UTILITY THEORY

We have already seen that the man in the airport example could have been regarded as acting on his belief that it was *likely* that his friend's plane would arrive at 2 p.m., in driving to the airport so as to arrive by 2 p.m. This is a particular instance of the general rule: *to act on the belief that a proposition is probable is very much the same as to act on the belief in the proposition.* Thus, it is clear that conclusions about probabilities profoundly affect behavior. However, this influence is more general than that which is encompassed in the formula above. The belief that one thing is *more probable than another,* though neither may be probable, may also affect action, for instance as such beliefs may affect the course of a search for a missing article. What is needed is a general theoretical account of the influence of probability judgments on behavior. Fortunately, this is just what is provided by the *expected utility theory* of decision making under risk, which can be regarded as being in some respects a generalization of Shwayder's picture of reason and action. Because of the importance of the expected utility theory to subsequent developments we describe it in some detail below, though the reader is referred to the literature of decision theory for a justification of its basic assumptions.[6]

The basic ideas of the expected utility theory are well illustrated in the following example, in which a man about to leave his house for the day is trying to decide whether to wear his raincoat or leave it behind. This is a *decision problem* in which the man must decide which of the following two *alternatives* to adopt:

$$A_1 = \text{to wear his raincoat}$$
$$A_2 = \text{to leave the raincoat at home.}$$

Note that while A_1 resembles an action 'proper' (in Shwayder's sense) in that some distinctive overt behavior is involved, A_2 is essentially to refrain from taking an action, which is clearly *not* an action 'proper'. Thus, while the alternatives decided among may include actions, not all of them need be.

Among the factors influencing the man's decision are his estimates of the likelihoods of two *contingencies*

$$C_1 = \text{that it should rain during the day}$$
and
$$C_2 = \text{that is should not rain during the day.}[7]$$

We may suppose the man's *probability estimates* for the two contingencies to be $p(C_1)$ and $p(C_2)$, which are assumed to be numbers between 0 and

1, summing to 1. Presumably if $p(C_1)$ is high (the man judges rain to be likely), then he will be likely to adopt alternative A_1, while if the $p(C_2)$ is high, he will be likely to adopt A_2.

Two other factors influencing the man's decision, besides the estimated probabilities of the contingencies, are his estimates of the *results* for him of adopting any alternative in each of the contingencies, and the *desirability* or undesirability of those results. For instance, if he thinks that the result of leaving the coat at home in the event that it rains will be that he will get a soaking, and he thinks it very undesirable to get soaked, then he will be more likely to take the coat than if he does not regard this result as particularly unpleasant. The two factors of *estimated result* and *desirability* are represented theoretically by the estimated result $R(A_i, C_j)$ expected to follow if A_i is adopted and contingency C_j arises, and by the numerical *utility* $u(R(A_i, C_j))$, which measures the degree of desirability of the estimated result $R(A_i, C_j)$. For instance, if the man estimates that he will get soaked if he leaves his coat behind (he adopts A_2) and it rains (contingency C_1 arises), and he regards that as excessively unpleasant, then $u(R(A_2, C_1))$ will be very low.

The thorny problem of attributing a clear sense to numerical utilities (as well as that of attaching a sense to numerical probability estimates), namely the *measurement problem*, is one which we shall not discuss here, though the works already cited, particularly Savage [17], discuss it in detail. For the sake of illustration, we shall simply assume here a 'plausible' set of numerical estimated probabilities and utilities, as follows:

$$p(C_1) = p(C_2) = \tfrac{1}{2}$$

and

$$u(R(A_1, C_1)) = -5$$
$$u(R(A_1, C_2)) = -2$$
$$u(R(A_2, C_1)) = -20$$
$$u(R(A_2, C_2)) = 5.$$

We assume in effect that the man estimates the chances of rain at 50%. The utilities of either of the possible results which might follow on the man's taking the coat (adopting alternative A_1) are assumed to be somewhat negative, that of the case in which it rains, C_1, being somewhat more disagreeable than that in which it does not rain, C_2. The utilities of the possible results which might follow on adopting A_2 – leaving the coat – are more disparate than are those of the possible results following on adoption of A_1. $R(A_2, C_1)$, the result of leaving the coat in the event of rain, is here represented as by far the worst of the various outcomes considered, while $R(A_2, C_2)$, the result of leaving the coat in the event of fair weather, is here represented as the only one of the possible results which is positively pleasurable.

The key 'law' of the expected utility theory is that a man estimating probabilities and desirabilities in the way outlined above will then adopt that alternative among all of the alternatives considered which has the *highest expected utility*. The expected utility of any alternative A_i is computed by multiplying each of the utilities of its possible results by the probability of the contingency leading to that result, and then adding together these products. In the present example, the expected utility of A_1, which we can denote '$u(A_1)$', is therefore equal to the product $u(R(A_1, C_1)) \times p(C_1)$ added to the product $u(R(A_1, C_2)) \times p(C_2)$. Thus, $u(A_1)$ is equal to $-5 \times \frac{1}{2} + -2 \times \frac{1}{2} = -3.5$. Computing $u(A_2)$ in the same way gives the sum $-20 \times \frac{1}{2} + 5 \times \frac{1}{2} = -7.5$. Therefore, since the expected utility $u(A_1)$ is higher than $u(A_2)$ (though both are negative), the man will adopt alternative A_1 according to the expected utility theory; i.e., he will wear his raincoat.

Though we shall not consider the justification for the apparently arbitrary 'formula' that persons adopt alternatives with the highest expected utilities,[8] it is possible to show that it agrees at least qualitatively with what we would intuitively expect. One special case, for instance, is that in which the decision maker regards one contingency as certain, so that its probability is estimated as 1, while the probability of any other contingency is estimated as 0. In this case the expected utility of any alternative is equal to the utility of that result which is certain would follow on adopting it, so the law that the decision maker adopts the alternative with the highest expected utility reduces to the plausible rule that he adopts the alternative whose estimated result is most desired (this is very close to our original formula that to act on the belief that a proposition is probable is very nearly the same as to act on the belief in the proposition). Another special case is that in which the possible results of adopting alternatives are classified as either *success* or *failure* (to attain some objective), where no way of succeeding is better than any other (and the same holds for failing), and where succeeding is assumed to be more desirable than failing. In this case it is easily seen that the alternative with the highest expected utility is simply the one which has the highest probability of resulting in success, and the 'maximize expected utility' rule simplifies to the rule to maximize the probability of success.

The special case just described shows that the expected utility theory of decision can be regarded as being in some ways a generalization of Shwayder's theory. The *purposes* which explain action in Shwayder's theory can be regarded as analogous to the aim of securing most desirable results, motivating the adoption of the alternative with the highest expected utility. That *degrees of desirability* are brought explicitly into account in the latter is a complication not present in the Shwayder theory. Similarly, the estimated likelihoods of occurrence of contingencies are in some ways analogous to the *beliefs* on which actions are based in Shwayder's account. *Degree of likelihood* represents an added complexity. Note too that attributing utilities to the possible results of acting and estimated likelihoods to these results can serve the same basic explanatory function which Shwayder supposes the ascription of purpose and belief to serve.

Two essentially new features of the expected utility theory are its considering *alternatives* which may not be actions, and *decisions* which, even if they issue in actions, are not the same as these actions. The latter innovation is especially important because, as suggested at the end of the previous section, considering the consequences of making *decisions* on the basis of beliefs may make it possible to evaluate the 'goodness' of kinds of beliefs which do not ordinarily issue in actions. Our example of the man deciding whether to wear his raincoat can be modified to illustrate this. Suppose the man had believed that it would not rain on the given day. As we have noted, this belief would have led him to leave his raincoat behind. If this belief were wrong, however, and it did rain on the given day, the result for him would have been to get soaked (we have assumed), which would not have happened if he had correctly concluded that it would rain on the day. Though the result of holding the negative belief in this case is not to take an *action* with unfortunate consequences, it is still to make a *decision* with unfortunate consequences, and this illustrates the utilitarian disadvantage of being wrong about a negative conclusion.

Now we want to consider the utilitarian advantages and disadvantages of arriving at better or worse estimates of probabilities.

4. A MOTIVE FOR WANTING TO ARRIVE AT CORRECT PROBABILITY ESTIMATES[9]

Assuming conclusions about probabilities to have the influence on decision and action characterized in the expected utility theory, people should have the best of utilitarian reasons for wanting to arrive at correct ones. These would in turn motivate concern for the soundness of reasoning leading to such conclusions. Or so it would seem. But if we consider more closely acting on conclusions as to the probabilities of events whose 'objective probabilities' are generally agreed on, it appears at first sight impossible to explain on utilitarian grounds why people should *want* to be right about them.

Accepting the expected utility picture of the connection between alternatives, contingencies and results, it is clear that if a person knew in advance which contingency would ultimately arise, the best alternative to adopt would be the one leading to the best result 'under the circumstances': i.e., in the contingency actually arising. Estimates of probabilities which would lead the person to choose this 'best-under-the circumstances' alternative would therefore be best when judged from the utilitarian point of view. But it is easily seen that the probability estimates which would lead a person to adopt the best-under-the-circumstances alternative would be precisely those which assigned probability 1 in advance to the contingency ultimately arising and probability 0 to all contingencies not ultimately arising. Call this probability assignment the 'lucky' one. Expected utility theory then entails that the most *fortunate* conclusion to arrive at about the probabilities of a set of contingencies is the lucky one. But it is evident that the most fortunate probability estimates are not always the same as the 'objective probabilities' – for instance as to a coin's falling heads when flipped on a particular occasion, which is generally assumed to be $\frac{1}{2}$, though the lucky probability estimate is necessarily either 0 or 1.

The foregoing result – that the most fortunate probability estimate is the lucky one – also agrees well with intuition. The man who, no matter how irrationally, can correctly guess what the future holds and act on his guesses is better off than the man who cannot, even though the latter's probability estimates may be more 'rational'.[10] If the consequences both of the expected utility theory and intuition are to be accepted, though, we are left without any apparent utilitarian reason for wanting to estimate probabilities correctly (in particular in such a way as to agree with the generally accepted probabilities connected with random phenomena).

Before trying to isolate a pragmatic value which might attach to correctly estimating the probabilities of contingencies whose 'true probabilities' can be calculated (e.g., that the points on two dice will total four when the dice are rolled, which is a contingency about whose probability it is easy to be mistaken), it is worth noting that it is often the case that when an effort is made to estimate probabilities something close to the lucky estimate is aimed for. The familiar example of weather forecasts couched in probabilistic terms (e.g., 'the chance of rain tomorrow is 30%') is arguably a case in point. There is clearly *a* sense in which weather forecasters aim to estimate rain as probable (say for the following day) on days when rain actually ensues, and as improbable on days when rain does not ensue. Assuming that persons act on these forecasts (say in deciding whether to wear their raincoats) as the expected utility theory says they do, they have good reason to *want* weather forecasters to be 'as accurate as possible' in this sense.[11] In fact it is hardly plausible that people with practical decisions to make would bother with such weather forecasts (or be willing to pay the forecasters) if they did not have reason to think that the forecasters were trying to come as close as possible to approximating the lucky forecast. If we look more closely at what the foregoing 'as close as possible' might mean, a way out of the dilemma into which we have gotten ourselves in trying to find a utilitarian value in estimating probabilities correctly suggests itself.

It is undeniable that there is a sense of 'best off' in which we feel that people are 'best off' estimating, say, the probability of rolling points totalling four with two dice as 1 in 12 (this being the theoretically correct probability). This in spite of the fact that we know that it is possible to be still better off estimating this event to have probability 1 prior to its occurrence, on all occasions when it actually does occur, and to have probability 0 on all other occasions. Plausibly the reason in this: though the logically best estimates to make (consistent with the expected utility theory) are the lucky ones, it is not practically possible to be lucky all of the time. If we take into account practical limitations on how often it is possible to be right or 'lucky' in the long run in predicting certain kinds of occurrences, it may be possible to explain why people are best guided 'in the long run' to estimate probabilities agreeing with the theoretically correct ones, and acting on those estimates. We shall see in a moment that the rationality of acting on the basis of 'objective' probabilities can be partially explained along these lines, but first let us note that 'good' probabilistic weather forecasts do contain implicit information as to how lucky it is possible to be in making weather forecasts under particular circumstances.

Consider what can be reasonably inferred on reading the forecast 'the chance of rain tomorrow is 30%,' in the evening newspaper. An obvious inference is that there is good reason to believe that on 30% of occasions similar to that in which the forecast was made, rain actually occurs on the following day. The sense of the word 'similar' here is one which the forecasters themselves could spell out to an extent, citing barometer readings, wind conditions, reported meteorological patterns, and so on, and the inference would be that when *these* conditions prevail rain occurs during the succeeding 24 hours 30% of the time. The second plausible inference is that no known method of weather forecasting relying on information known or 'available' to the forecasters at the time of forecasting could be expected to be right more than 30% of the time in the long run in predictions of the form 'it will rain tomorrow' made on occasions similar to the present one (e.g., with the same meteorological patterns as those presently prevailing, etc.). It is the second inference which tells us something about how often it is possible to be right or 'lucky' in making weather forecasts under similar circumstances. Also it is this which distinguishes probabilistic weather forecasts from simple relative frequency statements, which is a point worth further remark.

Note that if all that could be inferred from the forecast of a 30% chance of rain on the morrow was that on 30% of similar occasions rain actually occurs the following day (or that there is strong reason to think this is so), then in any region in which it rained 30% of all days every year it would be legitimate to make the prediction '30% probability of rain tomorrow' every day of the year, *meaning* that rain follows such days 30% of the time. But our 'unpredictability' inference could not be drawn from such predictions. For, granted what we do know about weather predicting, we know that in regions where it rains on 30% of the days of the year, it is possible to be right *more* than 30% of the time in making the prediction 'it will rain tomorrow', if present meteorological knowledge is utilized to 'select' the days on which this prediction is made. But this is just what we have reason to think can't be done to 'beat' good weather forecasts such as that the chance of rain tomorrow is 30%. Roughly, on occasions when forecasters make this prediction, we could not use the knowledge available at the time of forecasting to select from among those occasions ones on which to make the 'it will rain tomorrow' forecast, and reasonably expect to be right more than 30% of the time.[12]

Observe that the unpredictability inference which can be made from probabilistic weather forecasts is much more strongly justified from probabilistic statements about random occurrences: e.g., that the probability that the points will total four when two dice are rolled is 1 in 12. We have centuries of experience with dice and similar apparatus to justify our concluding that no matter how we try, there is no 'practical' way of making predictions of the form 'the points on the dice will total four' which will be right in the long run more (or less) than one time in twelve.[13]

We now want to give a plausible argument to the effect that if the 'unpredictability inference' from the weather forecast '30% probability of rain tomorrow' is warranted, then persons cannot do better in the long run than base their decisions on this estimate, assuming these decisions to be made on the basis of information available to the forecasters. Let us consider solely decisions made on occasions when this forecast is made, which are based on estimates of the likelihood or rain (which need not agree with the weather bureau's) and which issue in actions whose good or bad results depend only on whether or not it rains. To simplify, suppose we restrict attention to decisions as to whether or not a person (the decision maker) will wear his raincoat on leaving the house for the day, as previously discussed. To vastly oversimplify, suppose that the utilities for the decision maker of the possible results of his decision are always equal to those described in Section 3, and that, though his estimates of the probability of rain vary from day to day, they are always, absurdly, based only on information available to the weather bureau at the time it makes its forecasts. Recall that the utilities of the four possible results were: (1) -5 if the coat is worn and it rains, (2) -2 if the coat is worn and it doesn't rain, (3) -20 if the coat is not worn and it rains, and (4) $+5$ if the coat is not worn and it doesn't rain.

The first thing to observe is that for the decision maker to adopt the alternative of wearing the coat is for him to 'act as though' he predicted rain. Wearing the coat is the 'right' alternative to adopt in the event of rain, since the result of adopting it in that event has a higher utility (namely -2) than the result of not adopting it (which is -20). It is extremely plausible, then, that any limitations on how often the decision maker could correctly make the prediction 'it will rain' on a given set of occasions would apply equally to how often he would be 'right' on any subset of those occasions on which he would decide to wear the raincoat.

Now suppose that there are a total of N occasions on which the weather bureau makes the forecast 'the probability of rain is 30%', and that on N_1 of *these* the decision maker decides to wear his raincoat. Assuming that the weather bureau's prediction is 'best', it follows that the decision maker's decision to wear the raincoat would be right on only 30% of the N_1 occasions on which he wore the raincoat. This decision would be wrong, therefore, on 70% of the N_1 occasions of wearing the raincoat. By parallel reasoning, out of a total of $N_2 = N - N_1$ occasions on which it is decided not to wear the raincoat, *this* decision will be the right one to make on 70% of the N_2 occasions on which it is made, and the wrong one to make on 30% of those occasions. Assuming as we have done that the utility of the result of deciding 'rightly' to wear the coat is -5 (this being the utility of the result of wearing the coat in the event of rain) and that the utilities of the other results, right or wrong, are as given, the total 'net utility' of the result of wearing the coat N_1 times and leaving it behind N_2 times out of the total of N occasions on which the weather bureau's forecast is a 30% probability of rain will be:

$$- 5 \times .3N_1 + - 2 \times .7N_1 + - 20 \times 3N_2 + 5 \times .7N_2$$

which readily simplifies to:

$$- 2.9N_1 + - 2.5N_2 .$$

It is evident, since the total $N = N_1 + N_2$ is fixed, that the total net utility to the decision maker will be a maximum if he *never* wears the coat on any of the N occasions, so that $N_1 = 0$ and $N_2 = N$.

Whether the decision maker actually does wear his raincoat on any of the N occasions on which the weather bureau predicts a 30% probability of rain depends on the probabilities which the decision maker estimates for rain on those days (which may vary from day to day). If his estimate of the probability of rain on a given day is p, then the expected utility of the alternative of taking the raincoat is $-5p+-2(1-p)$, and the expected utility of not taking the raincoat is $-20p+5(1-p)$. It follows by simple algebra that the first expected utility is greater than the second, so the decision maker will take the raincoat, if p is greater than .316, while the expected utility of leaving the raincoat is the larger, and the raincoat will not be worn, if p is less than .316. Hence, if there is any occasion at all on which the decision maker estimates the probability of rain at more than .316, he will wear his coat, with the result that his net utility will be lower than the maximum attainable resulting from these decisions made on the N occasions.

The foregoing argument shows that if the decision maker ever estimates probabilities of rain as significantly *more* than 30% (in particular more than .316) when the weather bureau forecasts a 30% probability of rain, he will end up less well off 'in the long run' than if he does not. An entirely parallel argument shows that he will wind up less well off then he could be if he ever estimates probabilities of rain at significantly less than 30% on occasions when the weather bureau forecasts a 30% chance of rain. Hence the decision maker is best off estimating the chances of rain as 30% on those occasions.

Before turning to the possible implications which the foregoing has for soundness considerations, let us comment briefly on the aim of 'maximizing long term gains' as a motive for decision and action, which our argument suggests may partly explain why people should want to be 'right' in their conclusions about probabilities. There is no doubt that an adequate theory of behavior would have to take such motives into account, though it is probably an empirical matter how important they are. For instance, even the dog's behavior in the digging example might more plausibly be explained not as that of finding a bone on that particular occasion (as though *that* were all that mattered to the dog) but rather as part of a 'program of action designed to yield him a sufficient number of bones' (assuming him to be dependent on bones for food).

It is evident that though the aim of securing long run gains may motivate the desire to know 'true probabilities' it does not account for all of people's practical concern with probabilities. For example, in life and death cases where all that matters is the outcome of a single decision, people do seek information as to the probabilities involved, and we feel that they are 'best advised' to do so. Thus, a person suffering from a possibly mortal illness which might be cured by a new medicine which in turn is known to occasionally have lethal side effects will want to know what the chances of the medicine's curing him are, what the chances are of his recovering without taking the medicine, and what the chances are of its having its unfortunate side effects, before he makes up his mind. The problem which we haven't been able to solve here is the theoretical one of explaining why persons should *want* to know the true probabilities in theses cases.[14]

A final remark is in order concerning our equating the 'net utility' of the results of a long series of decisions with the *sum* of the utilities of the results of the individual decisions of the series. This assumption is suspect for two reasons, first because it presupposes that we can give a clear sense to even *comparing* the utilities of the results of two different decisions, and second because there are well known examples which show that the arithmetic summation assumption is sometimes highly counterintuitive. In fact, the expected utility theory was developed in large part in order to avoid both of the foregoing difficulties, and we are here using it in a way which leads right back to them. If our earlier comment that an adequate theory of behavior *must* consider the effect on behavior of long range goals is right, then it would follow that an adequate theory of behavior cannot avoid dealing with the problem of relating long range and short range values. On the other hand, it is extremely probable that an adequate theory will show that this relation is much more complicated than we have presently assumed it to be.

Now we want to see what light our partial explanation of the desirability of being right in estimating probabilities of factual propositions like 'it will rain tomorrow' throws on the question as to the relation between truth-conditional and probabilistic soundness for inferences involving only propositions of this kind. It is to be noted immediately that the partial explanation gives a motive for wanting to arrive at factual conclusions only under circumstances when they are objectively probable, and this in turn gives a motive for wanting to assure the probabilistic soundness of inferences issuing in such conclusions. For instance, if the conclusion 'it will rain tomorrow' is arrived at and acted on only under circumstances in which its objective probability is 95%, it would follow that these actions were 'the best under the circumstances' 95% of the time – because rain actually would follow 95% of the time.[15]

That truth-conditional soundness insures probabilistic soundness for inferences involving only factual propositions can be seen by considering the inference:

> It will either rain or snow tomorrow. It will not snow tomorrow. Therefore it will rain tomorrow.

Let us assume the truth-conditional soundness of the inference, hence that on any occasions in which the predictions 'it will either rain or snow tomorrow' and 'it will not snow tomorrow' proved correct (because it either rained or snowed, but it didn't snow the following day), the conclusion 'it will rain tomorrow' would prove correct. Now suppose that on some occasion both premises had probabilities of 95%; under those circumstances it would neither rain nor snow the following day 5% of the time, and also it would snow the following day only 5% of the time. Hence, under those circumstances at most 10% of the time *either* it would neither rain nor snow, *or* it would snow – i.e., under those circumstances one or other of the 'premise predictions' would be mistaken at most 10% of the time. Hence *both* premise predictions would be right at least 90% of the time, and so the conclusion would be right at least 90% of the time. Thus, if the premises have objective probabilities of 95%, then the conclusion has a probability of at least 90%, and we have already seen that this is the best that truth-conditional soundness *can* guarantee.

Observe that the foregoing argument made essential use of the connection between 'objective probabilities' and best attainable frequencies of correct predictability. This is precisely what cannot be shown (at any rate in any simple way) in the case of conditionals and objective estimates of their probabilities. This is the subject of the following three sections.

5. ACTING ON BELIEFS ABOUT THE RESULTS OF POSSIBLE ACTIONS[10]

The conclusions expressible as conditionals of concern in this section are ones as to what *result* will follow if a particular *alternative* is adopted by the person arriving at the conclusion. Examples of such *result beliefs* are:

If I take this medicine, my headache will go away.

and

If I eat those mushrooms, I will be poisoned.

It is intuitively obvious that beliefs of this type very strongly influence behavior, and the most immediately plausible way to describe this influence is to say that a person believing 'If I adopt alternative A then result R will follow' adopts A if he wants R, and does not adopt A if he does not want R. For instance, the man wanting to get rid of his headache and thinking that taking a particular medicine will do that takes the medicine, while the man not wanting to be poisoned who thinks he will be poisoned if he eats certain mushrooms does not eat the mushrooms. Ascribing these motives (to arrive at or avoid result R) and these beliefs (that if A is adopted R will follow) would also serve to explain the behavior (of adopting or not adopting A) in a manner analogous to that in which Shwayder supposes the ascription of motive and belief to explain behavior.

Somewhat closer examination of the possible explanatory function of the ascription of motive and belief shows that the simple way of describing the influence of motives and result beliefs on action above is incomplete in an essential respect. It would not do to explain a person's taking a particular medicine to cite solely his aim of getting rid of his headache and his belief that taking the medicine would have this desired result, if it were not tacitly supposed that the person taking the medicine *also* thought that if he did *not* take the medicine, his headache would *not* go away (or at any rate, would not go away so quickly). Similarly, in explaining why someone does not eat certain mushrooms on the grounds of that person's belief that he will be poisoned if he eats them, it is tacitly assumed that the person thinks that he will not be poisoned if he doesn't eat the mushrooms. Making these tacitly assumed beliefs explicit leads to the following rather more complicated picture of the influence of sets of result beliefs on behavior. A person is supposed to decide which of mutually exclusive and exhaustive alternatives $A_1, ..., A_n$ to adopt, and for each alternative A_i to hold a belief to the effect that if A_i is adopted, then result R_i will follow. He then adopts whichever alternative A_i has the most desirable anticipated result R_i. For instance, in the mushroom example, the man 'adopts the alternative' of not eating the mushrooms because he thinks that the result of that (not to be poisoned) is better than the result of adopting the other alternative (which he thinks would be to be poisoned).

Given the great practical importance of result beliefs, it would seem as in the case of conclusions about probabilities that people should have the strongest of motives for wanting to be 'right' in them. However, it turns out to be difficult to characterize a sense of 'right' and 'wrong' applicable to such conclusions which can be closely connected to people's practical interests in reasoning which issues in them, in that they would generally be better off basing their decisions on result beliefs which would be 'right' in this sense than in basing them on ones which were 'wrong'. Observe first that the fact that the consequence beliefs on which decisions are based ultimately turn out to be 'materially true' by no means guarantees that these conclusions are the 'best' to arrive at and that the decision maker would not have done better to arrive at other conclusions and to act differently in consequence. Suppose that the mushrooms which the man avoided eating because he thought that if he did so he would be poisoned had been non-poisonous, and in fact delicious. Not eating the mushrooms 'made' his belief 'if I eat the mushrooms I will be poisoned' materially true, and therefore he was 'right' in the sense of holding a belief which was materially true. But it is evident that if the man had not arrived at this conclusion he would in fact have made a decision with better consequences – namely to eat the delicious and non-poisonous mushrooms. He can hardly therefore regard the reasoning which led him to the conclusion 'if I eat those mushrooms I will be poisoned' as satisfactory simply because the conclusion he arrived at was materially true. This of course only confirms our strong intuitive feeling that merely turning out to be materially true does not prove the rightness of the belief 'if I eat those mushrooms I will be poisoned'.[17]

Trying to explain what more in the way of 'rightness' should be wanted of consequence conclusions beyond that they should be materially true seems to lead us inevitably to counterfactuals with all of their attendant problems. For example, we are most apt to describe the man in the mushroom example as having been wrong in thinking 'If I eat these mushrooms I will be poisoned' (when the mushrooms are actually non-poisonous) by saying that in fact, he *would not* have been poisoned if he had eaten the mushrooms.[18] It is not to be thought that we can easily avoid the counterfactual and attach a 'factual' sense to an 'adequate' concept of rightness or wrongness as it applies to conditionals. The reason is that it appears to be necessary to use the counterfactual even to define what the 'best' alternative to adopt under certain circumstances is, which would in turn permit us to characterize 'right' consequence conclusions as being ones which we should want to arrive at since basing our decisions on them leads to adopting the best alternatives. Thus, not eating the mushrooms in the example was characterized as not being the best alternative to adopt (in the circumstance in which the mushrooms are in fact non-poisonous), since eating the mushrooms *would have* been pleasurable, and would have had no harmful after-effects.

Assuming that the problem of characterizing 'best' consequence conclusions to come to brings us inevitably to the counterfactual, we shall not pursue this subject further here, particularly in view of the fact that this difficulty can be avoided in dealing with the problem of characterizing 'best' conclusions to arrive at about the *probabilities* of such propositions. It is worth noting by way of conclusion, however, that taking seriously the fact that 'best' conclusions and actions are fundamentally described in counterfactual terms, leads us to see that certain non-necessary 'causal' counterfactual assumptions are presupposed even in our earlier account of why it is best to arrive at and act on correct conclusions about matters of fact. For instance, in the example of the man deciding whether to wear his raincoat, we have assumed that the 'right' and 'best' conclusion for him to arrive at in circumstances in which rain actually does ensue is that it *will* rain. Acting on this by taking the raincoat was said to be best because the result of adopting the other alternative – to leave the raincoat at home – would have been less desirable under the circumstances than the result of taking the coat. But this claim really rests on the assumption that taking the coat has no influence on the weather, and in particular that this action is not what 'brings on' the rain. If, absurdly, carrying the coat had been what brought on the rain, then it was correct to conclude in advance that it would rain, but it no longer follows that acting on this conclusion by carrying the raincoat has a better result than would have followed if the opposite conclusion had been arrived at and the coat left behind. It may still be possible in the case in which conclusions lead to actions which influence the events to which the conclusions pertain, to give a coherent description of what 'best' and 'right' conclusions to arrive at are, but we may plausibly suppose that this description will involve counterfactuals in an essential way, and we will be back in the difficulties to which we are led in attempting to characterize 'best conclusions' about result propositions.

Taking into account the possibility of action influencing the 'contingencies' entering into the simple expected utility theory outlined in Section 3 will be seen to call into question our characterization of 'luckiest' probability estimates. This emerges when we consider this theory as a special case of a theory of decision and action based on estimates of the probabilities of possible results of actions, which we now take up.

6. ACTING ON ESTIMATES OF THE PROBABILITIES OF THE POSSIBLE CONSEQUENCES OF ACTIONS

If the man in our mushroom example had only regarded it as 'not improbable' that he would be poisoned if he ate the mushrooms, this would no doubt have deterred him from eating them fully as effectively as if he had believed 'if I eat these mushrooms I will be poisoned' *simpliciter*. A natural and obvious simultaneous generalization of the expected utility theory and of our theory of action on sets of result beliefs provides an elegant description of the effect on behavior of estimates as to the probabilities of certain results following on the adoption of various alternatives. Where persons regard more than one result as possible following the adoption of a particular alternative, it can be supposed that they attach probabilities to the occurrence of these results if the alternative is adopted, and also utilities. These probabilities and utilities then permit the calculation of the *expected utility* of adopting the alternative, according to the rule described in Section 3. Finally, it is natural to assume that the alternative adopted is the one with the highest expected utility. For instance, in the mushroom example we may suppose that the person thinks there is one chance in 100 that he will be poisoned if he eats the mushrooms and that he attaches a utility of $-10,000$ to this, while he thinks that there are 99 chances in 100 that he won't be poisoned, and the utility of this is $+10$. The expected utility of eating the mushrooms is then equal to $.01 \times -10,000 + .99 \times 10 = -90.1$. Assuming this value to be lower than the expected utility of not eating the mushrooms, the person will not eat the mushrooms.

Generalizing from the mushroom example, the influence of beliefs about the probabilities of possible results following on the adoption of various alternatives can be described as follows. It is assumed that one of the mutually exclusive and exhaustive alternatives $A_1, ..., A_n$ must be adopted. For each alternative A_i, instead of supposing that there is a unique result R_i which it is expected would follow from it, there are n_i possible results $R_1, ..., R_{n_i}$ which are thought might follow if A_i is adopted. Each of these is regarded as having a probability of following *if* A_i is adopted, and these *conditional probabilities* can therefore be written as $p(A_i \Rightarrow R_{i1}), ..., p(A_i \Rightarrow R_{in_i})$. For fixed A_i the foregoing probabilities can be assumed to sum to 1, corresponding to the fact that $R_{i1}, ..., R_{in_i}$ are regarded as mutually exclusive and exhaustive possible results which could follow adopting A_i. Also, a numerical utility is supposed to be attached to result R_{ij}'s following on the adoption of A_i, and this too can be represented as a *conditional utility*, $u(A_i \Rightarrow R_{ij})$. The expected utility of adopting A_i, which can be denoted $u(A_i)$, is then simply taken to be the sum of the products $p(A_i \Rightarrow R_{ij}) \times u(A_i \Rightarrow R_{ij})$ with j running from 1 to n_i.

Before touching on certain conceptual problems connected with the foregoing description of the influence of 'result probability estimates' on behavior, let us note how both the expected utility theory of Section 3 and the representation of action on the basis of consequence beliefs described in Section 4 can be regarded as special cases of the present 'model'. The case in which the decision maker regards each possible alternative as having a unique result R_i is essentially that in which for each A_i there is one possible result R_{ij_i} in the set $R_{i1}, ..., R_{in_i}$ such that $p(A_i \Rightarrow R_{ij_i})$ is 1, while $p(A_i \Rightarrow R_{ij})$ is 0 for all j different from j_i. In this case the expected utility $u(A_i)$ reduces just to the conditional utility $u(A_i \Rightarrow R_{ij_i})$, and therefore the decision maker adopts whichever alternative A_i whose expected result R_{ij_i} has the highest value.

The expected utility model of Section 3 can be regarded as the special case in which: (1) the conditional probabilities $p(A_i \Rightarrow R_{ij})$ are computable from 'subconditional probabilities' of R_{ij}'s following if A_i is adopted *and* a contingency C_k arises, and (2) the contingencies C_k are 'independent' of the alternative adopted. Briefly summarized, the argument is as follows. Suppose that there are m possible 'contingencies' $C_1, ..., C_m$. It follows from the pure axioms of conditional probability that $p(A_i \Rightarrow R_{ij})$ is equal to the sum of the products $p(A_i \Rightarrow C_k) \times p(A_i \ \& \ C_k \Rightarrow R_{ij})$ for k running from 1 to m. If the contingencies C_k are regarded as 'causally independent' of the alternative adopted A_i, then we can write $p(A_i \Rightarrow C_k) = p(C_k)$. If the alternative A_i and the contingency C_k are regarded as uniquely determining the result R_{ij}, this means that for each A_i and C_k there is a unique result $R(A_i, C_k)$ such that $p(A_i \ \& \ C_k \Rightarrow R_{ij})$ is 1 if R_{ij} is $R(A_i, C_k)$, and $p(A_i \ \& \ C_k \Rightarrow R_{ij})$ is 0 otherwise. It follows from these assumptions that the expected utility $u(A_i)$ is equal to the sum of the products $p(C_k) \times u(A_i \Rightarrow R(A_i, C_k))$. Note that the utility $u(A_i \Rightarrow R(A_i, C_k))$ is really the same as the utility $u(R(A_i, C_k))$ in the earlier model, since in that model this was assumed to represent the value of the result $R(A_i, C_k)$ following if A_i was adopted and C_k occurred.

Observe the light in which our present generalization puts our earlier representation of the result $R(A_i, C_k)$ as a *function* of the alternative A_i adopted and the contingency C_k arising. $R(A_i, C_k)$ is now seen to be the result which the decision maker *thinks* is certain will follow if A_i is adopted and C_k occurs. But the fact that he thinks this does not mean that $R(A_i, C_k)$ *must* follow – he could be mistaken. In fact this possibility is very real in our earlier representation of 'getting soaked' as the result of leaving the raincoat in the event of rain. The man could be mistaken about that since it is certainly possible to avoid being soaked even when it rains and the coat is left behind. If the uncertainties as to the results of adopting alternatives in various contingencies which are tacit in the simple expected utility model are made explicit, we are in fact led right back to the more general expected utility picture formulated here. Furthermore making these uncertainties explicit and allowing for the possibility of error in estimating the result of adopting an alternative in some contingency calls into question our characterization of the 'lucky' probability estimate as being that which assigns probability 1 to the contingency ultimately occurring. The following example illustrates this.

Suppose a miner prospecting for silver to be considering whether to dig in a particular location. He estimates that if he digs and there is actually silver to be found, he will have a 'good' result, while if he digs and silver is not to be found, he will have a poor one (he will have tired himself out and wasted his efforts). He would prefer not to dig rather than dig fruitlessly. His decision whether to dig is therefore based on his estimate of the probability of there being silver to be found. Now, suppose that there actually isn't silver to be found, but there is gold. The miner would not be luckiest to be 'right' in estimating silver as certain not to be found (which is what we have previously taken to be the 'lucky' probability estimate under the circumstances) since this would lead him not to dig, although digging would actually have led him to the gold. What this example shows is that regarding the 'right' probability estimate as the lucky one really presupposes that the results of adopting alternatives in various contingencies are *correctly* estimated. In particular we must assume that the miner is right in estimating that the result of digging and not finding silver will be 'poor'. The possibility of being mistaken in these estimates is left out of account where they are represented as 'givens' (which is how they are construed in the expected utility model of Section 3). When this possibility is taken into account we are led to difficulty in defining 'luckiest' probability estimates analogous to those which arise in trying to characterize 'best' conclusions about the consequences of adopting alternatives, which were noted in the previous section. For this reason we shall not even try to define a generalization of our earlier 'lucky' probability estimates applicable to the present model, when we come to consider what 'best' consequence probability estimates are. Before turning to that we conclude with brief remarks on conceptual problems arising in connection with the present generalized expected utility theory.

The basic conceptual problem which must be solved if our generalized theory of decision based on consequence probability estimates is to be given a clear sense (which would in turn permit it to be evaluated) is to specify the meanings of the numerical utilities and probability estimates entering into the definition of expected utility. This is the *measurement problem*, which we asserted in Section 3 to be solvable in a satisfactory way within the context of the 'special expected utility theory', though we did not discuss that solution. One thing to be observed here is that the measurement problem cannot be solved within the generalized theory in the same way that it can in the special theory though it turns out a solution of the same general type is possible. The solution in the context of the special theory consists in attaching a 'behavioral' sense to numerical utilities and probabilities, by specifying what purely 'qualitative' behavior by people can be interpreted as 'acting as though' they attached particular probabilities to propositions and numerical utilities to possible results.

This behavioral interpretation of probability and utility, however, actually is based on the assumption that the postulates of the special expected utility theory which relate probability and utility to decision are valid; in other words, the assumptions of the special theory are used as partial implicit definitions of its numerical concepts, and therefore the theory itself is interpreted as postulating that people act 'as though' they attached numerical probabilities and utilities to propositions and results, in their decision-making behavior. But, granted that the assumptions of the special theory are used as implicit definitions of utility and estimated probability, it follows that a theory which does not make these same assumptions, and in fact makes weaker ones, cannot necessarily use these as implicit definitions in the same way that the special theory does. In fact, this is the case with our generalized theory. It can be shown to be logically impossible to define utility and probability implicitly in terms of the assumptions of our general theory, *purely* in terms of preference and choice, as is done in the special theory.[19]

The 'implicit definition' approach can be used in the present context to give behavioral interpretations to numerical utility and estimated probability, provided 'behavior' is interpreted to include not only *preference* (either between alternatives, or between their possible results) but *qualitative likelihood comparisons* of the form 'if A_i is adopted, then R_{i1} is more likely to follow than R_{i2}'.[20] Of course, once the behavioral reduction of utility and estimated probability has been accomplished it still remains to be shown that persons do have good reason to behave in accord with the assumptions of the general theory as thus interpreted, at least to a first approximation. We shall not consider this problem in its usual form here (which is usually construed as that of deriving a 'representation theorem' from suitable 'axioms of rationality' – see, e.g., Krantz *et al.* [38]), since we will approach the subject of 'justification' from a different direction in the following section. What we want to show there is that, provided persons want to maximize long run gains, as measured by sums of individual utilities, they are 'best off' to estimate and act on consequence probabilities which are 'objective'. In arguing for this, however, we don't want to assume that the utilities involved are implicitly defined by the postulates of our generalized theory, because those postulates *assume*, in effect, the validity of the ratio representation of the probabilities of conditionals, and it is the correctness of this representation (in the sense that it is desirable to arrive at probability estimates conforming to it) which we now propose to argue for.

7. BEST ESTIMATES OF THE PROBABILITIES OF THE POSSIBLE RESULTS OF ACTIONS

Suppose a decision maker to make a long series of decisions in which on each occasion he must adopt one of alternatives $A_1, ..., A_n$, and where the possible results which could follow from adopting A_i are always among $R_{i1}, ..., R_{in_i}$. Suppose for simplicity's sake that the value to the decision maker of result R_{ij}'s following adopting A_i is always $u(A_1 \Rightarrow R_{ij})$, and that in a long series of results, the net value is equal to the sum of the values of the individual results in the series. Finally, suppose that decisions are made under circumstances in which, no matter how the decision maker 'selects' the occasions on which to adopt any particular alternative A_i, result R_{ij} will follow on adopting A_i a proportion $f(A_i, R_{ij})$ of the times in which A_i is adopted. It is easily seen that under these circumstances, if in a long series of N of these decisions each alternative A_i is adopted N_i times, the net utility of the results in the series must be close to the double sum:

$$N_1[f(A_1, R_{11}) u(A_1 \Rightarrow R_{11}) + \cdots + f(A_1, R_{1n_1}) u(A_1 \Rightarrow R_{1n_1})]$$
$$+ \cdots$$
$$N_n[f(A_n, R_{n1}) u(A_n \Rightarrow R_{n1}) + \cdots + f(A_n, R_{nn_n}) u(A_n \Rightarrow R_{nn_n})].$$

Assuming that the decision maker wants to maximize his long term gains, he will always choose that alternative A_i for which the value

$$f(A_i, R_{i1}) u(A_i \Rightarrow R_{i1}) + \cdots + f(A_i, R_{in_i}) u(A_i \Rightarrow R_{in_i})$$

is a maximum. His net gain will then be N times this value, where N is the total number of occasions on which the decision is made.

What the foregoing tends to show is that in situations in which 'objective long run frequency constraints' exist of the type postulated above, persons are best off in the long run always to adopt alternatives with highest expected utilities, where expected utilities are computed in terms of these frequencies. As the frequencies $f(A_i, R_{ij})$ necessarily satisfy the laws of the ratio representation, it follows that in making decisions in the type of situation described, persons are best off arriving at estimates of the probabilities of the possible consequences of alternatives which conform to the ratio representation, and then adopting alternatives with highest expected utilities as computed in terms of these probabilities. Though we should want to inquire how 'typical' the sort of decision making situation considered here is, we have now found *a* motive for wanting to reach 'right' conclusions about the probabilities of the possible consequences of actions, where these 'true probabilities' satisfy the ratio representation. We also have a motive for wanting to reach 'simple conditional conclusions' about the results of adopting alternatives only when they have high ratio probabilities, and therefore for wanting to assure the probabilistic soundness of inferences with such conditionals as conclusions. In particular, assuming people act on their 'simple result conclusions' in the way depicted in Section 5, they will arrive at best results in the long run if they conclude 'if I adopt A_i then R_i will follow' only under circumstances when the 'objective' ratio probability is high.

Note in conclusion the light which the foregoing throws on the connection between 'best' estimates of the probability of 'if I adopt A_i then R_i will follow' and possible truth-value ascriptions to this conditional. This rational estimate is equal to the frequency with which R_i follows the adoption of A_i under circumstances where it is not possible to 'be clever' and get result R_i more or less often in the long run in circumstances of that type. This frequency is therefore independent of the possible truth or falsity of conditional utterances of the form 'if I adopt A_i then R_i will follow' under conditions in which A_i is not adopted. Thus, the probability of the conditional is not to be equated with the frequency with which the conditional 'if I adopt A_i then R_i will follow' proves true (in some sense of 'true') on *all* occasions on which this assertion might be made, but rather only with the proportion of times the consequent would prove true on occasions when the conditional is asserted and its antecedent proves true. This confirms, then, the result arrived at in Section I.1 that, however we might ascribe truth-conditions to conditionals, we cannot in general expect that their probabilities can be equated with their probabilities of having the ascribed truth-value 'true'.

NOTES

[1] Though it is beside our present concerns, it seems to me that Dummett's contention is obviously wrong if taken in full generality (unless the word 'statement' is taken in a special technical sense) and to the extent it is right in limited generality, this is to be explained in terms of the desirability of reaching true conclusions 'for oneself', and not only in what one passes on to others. Note that while Dummett's attempt to analyze truth in terms of statement-making involves essential altruistic assumptions (in common with the *sincerity conditions* of speech acts of more general kinds, to which Dummett's claim is obviously closely connected), our approach does not require this.

[2] A somewhat more exact description of the action would be to say it was done in the belief that it was *probable* that the friend's plane would arrive close to 2 p.m. This complication will be taken up in the following section.

[3] Or at least that the action had a 'reasonable chance' of accomplishing the purpose; this modification is easily accomodated in the probabilistic generalization to follow.

[4] Perhaps the recent work of Zadeh [62], Goguen [21] and other of Zadeh's associates on the logic of 'fuzzy' or 'inexact' concepts can be regarded as a step in this direction. Zadeh and Bellman [63] have taken the further step of relating 'fuzzy conclusions' to decision and action in a way which might make it possible to ascribe motives for wanting to be 'fuzzily right'.

[5] I have taken some very limited steps towards developing a theory of that kind of soundness, using procedures somewhat analogous to those described in Chapters I and II to determine whether the fact that all generalizations of a set of 'premise generalizations' admit only a small proportion of exceptions insures that a conclusion of the same form also only admits a small proportion of exceptions. The results appear in [4]. See also Carlstrom [10].

[6] The classical references are de Finetti [13], Ramsey [45], Savage ([47], Chapter 1) and von Neumann and Morgenstern ([61], Chapter 1). A lucid critical discussion appears in Luce and Raiffa ([42], Chapter 2), and the theory has received a great deal of attention in the literatures of statistical decision theory, and of behavioral sciences such as experimental psychology and economics. Philosophical literature, connecting this with the foundations of probability, is also extensive. The present formulation differs slightly from standard formulations, by way of emphasizing the fact that utilities apply to *expected* results of adopting alternatives under various circumstances. That these expectations themselves are subject to some uncertainty will prove important when we come to generalize the present considerations in such a way as to account for acting on the basis of estimated *conditional* probabilites.

[7] This oversimplifies, of course, since the man would also consider how hard it might rain, and for how long. These refinements can be taken into account without complicating the theory in an essential way.

[8] The justification of this rule is clearly intimately bound up with the problem of defining or measuring subjective probabilities and utilities, for if the method of measuring the latter were to be varied, it would follow that expected utilities, which should be maximized in choosing among alternatives, could not be computed according to the formula here described. The question of justification will, however, arise in a new guise in the following section.

[9] Dealing with the issues of concern in this section compels us to confront the highly controversial problem of the 'meaning of probability'. The very limited 'solution' I shall propose to this problem will be seen to be highly unorthodox, and is certainly

not to be attributed to proponents of the expected utility theory to which it is closely bound. It will be seen in fact that it is necessary to give a somewhat unorthodox interpretation to some of the 'primitive concepts' of the latter theory in order to make possible an explanation as to why one should *want* to reach 'correct' conclusions about probabilities, assuming he acts on these conclusions in accord with the expected utility theory.

[10] This conclusion must be modified when we come to consider the possibility that people may be mistaken in their conclusions as to what the results of adopting particular alternatives will be in different contingencies. An example to be discussed later of a miner digging for silver and finding gold instead can be seen as a case in which acting on mistaken opinions actually leads to better results than would have followed if the alternative 'directed' by the *right* opinion had been adopted in the circumstances. This sort of situation cannot be accomodated within the expected utility framework previously described, but can be within the conditional generalization to be discussed in Section 6.

[11] It is an interesting problem to devise a rational measure of this kind of accuracy. One such, which is essentially an adaptation to the familiar negentropy measure of statistical information theory, has been used by Joseph Hanna [27], as a device for assessing the 'goodness' of predictions in probabilistic theories of learning.

[12] This is not to say that we couldn't do better than the professionals using information *not* available to them. For instance, looking at the skies on the following morning might give us practical certainty that it was going to rain that day, and in this case we would be better advised to rely on that information than we would be to act on the basis of the forecast probabilities. 'Up to the minute' forecasts are generally to be preferred. But information as to tomorrow's skies is precisely what is not available to forecasters making predictions the evening before, and it must also be remembered that action on expectations as to contingencies like the weather must be undertaken at *some* time prior to the occurrence of the events which the expectations relate to.

Two further comments on our somewhat tortuous second inference from the probabilistic weather prediction are worth making. One is that the 'information available' to the forecasters, while *not* including the look of the skies the next morning, does include items of 'potential information' which may not actually be used – for instance pronouncements previously made by astrologers which the scientific weather forecasters could consult if they chose to. That such potential items are not used shows that there is good reason to think that they would be useless.

The second comment is that we do not exclude the possibility that ways of forecasting may be developed which will 'beat' present methods, either relying on kinds of information not practically available to forecasters now (perhaps transmitted from improved weather satellites), or else by better analyzing data already available to forecasters. All that we have a right to conclude from the weather bureau's forecast is that among presently known ways of predicting (which include uneducated guesses after looking at the sky, *merely* looking at the barometer, and even less scientific methods), none can reasonably be expected to be better than the weather bureau's.

[13] This is the 'nonexistence of a gambling system' condition, which has been noted frequently as an essential feature of random processes. This requirement is not meant to exclude the possibility of being right more often than by chance, making predictions on the outcomes of such processes based on an exact specification of the initial conditions of the process: e.g., knowing the precise velocities, directions, weights, etc. of the dice when rolled would theoretically enable us to predict the result of the roll (leaving

aside quantum uncertainties anyway). But this 'initial condition' information is not practically available.

Another complication which we have neglected is the fact that theoretical statements about the probabilities of random phenomena are usually formulated as *generalizations* and not as propositions about singular occurrences – e.g., 'the chance of rolling points totalling four with two dice is 1 in 12'. It is to be conjectured that it is the fact that theoretical statements about probabilities are nearly always generalizations which has led the 'relative frequency' probability theorists to the view that probability statements are *never*, if they are legitimate, about particular occurrences.

14 This is connected with what seems to me to be an essential lack in Strawson's well known attempt to 'dissolve' the problem of induction, arguing in effect that it is a matter of what we mean by 'rational' that to have good reasons for certain opinions *is* to have good inductive support for them ([55], pp. 261–262). What Strawson does not tell us is why we should *want* to hold opinions which are 'rational' in his sense. We are again back at the basic difference in approach, between regarding issues of logic as matters to be settled by conceptual analysis (e.g., as to the meaning of the concept of rationality), and regarding them as ones to be studied by considering why persons should want to reach conclusions of one or another kind, where such words as 'rationality' may only very vaguely and crudely describe what is wanted.

15 That rain would follow 95% of the time can be inferred from the fact that under *these* circumstances (where the objective probability of rain is 95%), it is impossible to 'outguess' the objective probabilities, and make the prediction 'it will rain' correctly more or less than 95% of the time. It is necessary to use the assumed unpredictability in this case to assure that the *reasoner* will be right in his prediction 95% of the time he predicts rain when the true probability of rain is 95%. Otherwise the reasoner might be assumed able to 'alter the odds' and predict rain correctly either more or less than 95% of the time when he predicted rain under circumstances in which the true probability of rain is 95%.

16 I am indebted to Professor Donald Davidson for drawing my attention to the type of conclusion expressible as a conditional to be discussed in this section, which, among all conclusions of conditional form, probably have the strongest and most immediate influence on behavior. Conclusions about the results of possible actions of ones own (what we call a *result proposition*) might be considered to be too special a class of belief expressible as a conditional to justify drawing inferences about conditionals in general from this special case; Dummett [16], for instance, would appear to think so since he explicitly excludes conditionals whose 'antecedents are in the speaker's power' from his considerations. It would be very odd, however, if the special class differed from conditionals of other sorts so far as their truth-conditions and probabilities were concerned. In any case this particular kind of belief is of sufficient importance to justify detailed discussion in its own right.

In my earlier articles [1, 2] I had attempted to get at the pragmatic consequences of holding beliefs expressible as conditionals by regarding conditional *bets* as actions 'based on' these beliefs. While there is probably something right about this, bets in general involve such complicated linguistic behavior (and rely on conventions regarding their settlement which are so difficult to specify precisely) that it has seemed better to leave them out of account entirely here. The type of action on the basis of sets of consequence beliefs which we shall consider here is in general non-linguistic, and we may imagine such acts performed by animals.

17 There is a special case in which the fact that all beliefs of a 'consequence belief set'

are materially true is necessary and sufficient for actions based on them to have desirable results. This is that in which alternatives are evaluated solely in regard to whether they will result in some single purpose being achieved, so all consequence beliefs are of the form 'if I adopt A_i, purpose P will (will not) be achieved. Acting on these leads to the adopting of some alternative A_i which it is thought will lead to achieving the purpose. Trivially, all the conditionals of this set prove to be materially true under these conditions if and only if the purpose actually is achieved. We still would not want to say that 'arriving at conclusions which are materially true' aptly described the aim of reasoning about consequence propositions in this case, if only because this aim alone would not explain why we should regard it as unsatisfactory to arrive at 'probabilistically inconsistent conclusions' of the form 'if I adopt A_i then R_i will follow, and if I adopt A_i then R_i will not follow'. It is to be conjectured that what would be unsatisfactory about arriving at this type of 'inconsistency' would not so much be that actions based on them would have undesirable results, but rather that such conclusions cannot be acted on.

[18] Note the transition to the subjunctive 'after the fact' where the conditional 'If I eat these mushrooms I will not be poisoned' which might have been affirmed prior to deciding not to eat the mushrooms becomes 'subjunctivized' *a posteriori*. We will come upon a similar phenomenon in Chapter IV, where we consider the effect on the mood of the conditional 'if A then B' *a posteriori*, after learning 'not B'.

[19] Something like this difficulty also arises with Richard Jeffrey's theory of decision, formulated in his book *The Logic of Decision* [34]. The basic problem in Jeffrey's case is the same as that arising in ours: namely that he allows the possibility of action influencing probability (this is not explicit in Jeffrey's theory, since he makes no clear distinction between alternatives which are chosen among and 'events' of other kinds, but it is implicit). On the other hand, Jeffrey's theory makes certain 'combinatorial' assumptions which the present theory does not, and this permits a kind of 'reduction' of probability and utility to pure preference which is not possible in the present context.

[20] Actually, we must assume that these likelihood comparisons can be made not only between 'atomic results' like R_{i1} ans R_{i2}, but also among 'Boolean combinations' of them, so that a person can make a judgment of the form 'if A_i is adopted it is more likely that R_{i1} will follow than that one of R_{i2} or R_{i3} will follow'.

CHAPTER IV

A HYPOTHESIS CONCERNING COUNTERFACTUALS; PROBABILITY CHANGE ASPECTS OF INFERENCE

1. AN EPISTEMIC PAST TENSE INTERPRETATION OF COUNTERFACTUALS

The hypothesis with which this chapter is concerned is that, in a sense to be explained, counterfactual conditionals like

> If that bird were a canary then it would be yellow.

function as a kind of 'epistemic past tense', and in particular their probabilities at the time of utterance equal the probabilities which were or might have been attached to corresponding indicative conditionals like

> If that bird is a canary then it will be yellow.

on real or hypothetical prior occasions. This hypothesis, which was earlier advanced in Adams [5] and independently by Skyrms in [50], will prove in the end to be untenable or at best dubious in complete generality. Nevertheless, it offers simple and plausible explanations for such a wide variety of logical phenomena involving the counterfactual that it merits detailed consideration in that one may reasonably expect a hypothesis *like* the present one to be central to any satisfactory general theory of the counterfactual.

There is a difficulty in saying just what a counterfactual conditional *is*. Goodman [23], Michael Ayers [8], and the author [5] have all argued that it is a mistake to define counterfactuals as conditionals which entail or in some sense 'implicate' the falsity of their antecedents, and we will give below further reasons for rejecting the 'antecedent falsity' characterization. It is more plausible to identify the counterfactual with the *subjunctive mood* as in "if that bird were a canary it would be yellow", but this too is not entirely satisfactory. The subjunctive is also the standard mood of indirect discourse, as when one person reports another's conditional utterance "the meetings will be held indoors if it rains" by saying "he said that the meetings would be held indoors if it rained". Also we feel uneasy in calling a warning like "I would not do that if I were you" a counterfactual conditional (or *any* kind of conditional), just because of its employment of the "were... would not..." construction. Furthermore, we do not really know the limits of the subjunctive, and in the end we will see reasons for wanting to regard statements like

> Had he studied, he should have passed.

and even

> If he studied then he should have passed.

as counterfactuals, whether or not they are grammatically of subjunctive form. Given these difficulties, it is probably premature to attempt a precise characterization of 'the counterfactual conditional' (such a characterization might more properly be expected to *accompany* and not to preceed the formulation of an adequate theory of counterfactuals), and we will content ourselves here with the rough description of counterfactuals as being conditionals *like* "if that bird were a canary then it would be yellow."

Granted that counterfactuals do not necessarily entail the falsity of their antecedents, it is possible to argue that they do not in fact differ in logically essential respects from their corresponding indicative conditionals (Ayers [8] argues for the logical equivalence of the two forms). We now wish to argue that the two forms do differ logically but this difference is of a special sort, the characterization of which leads us to formulate our 'epistemic past tense' hypothesis. A typical situation in which the two conditionals differ is that in which their common consequent is known to be false, where the counterfactual is often affirmable while the indicative is not. Going back to our canaries, imagine the following situation. Two men are walking in the woods and spy a bird in the shadow in such a way that its color cannot be made out. One man might use the indicative in telling the other "If that bird is a canary it will be yellow." Now, however, suppose that the bird flies out into the sunlight, where it is clearly seen to be blue and not yellow. Under the circumstances the first man will be unlikely to continue to affirm the indicative – and indeed he should not, since learning the falsity of its consequent makes it too improbable to justify continued affirmation. On the other hand the first speaker will be likely to 'substitute the counterfactual for the indicative' and affirm "if that bird were a canary it would be yellow." It must be stressed that this 'finding the consequent to be false' type of situation is not one in which the indicative conditional is found to be *false* while the counterfactual is *true*, but rather one in which the *probability* of the indicative conditional becomes low as a result of learning new evidence (that its consequent is false), while presumably the probability of the counterfactual is high or becomes high. Our problem is to substantiate the latter claim, by giving a theoretical representation of the probabilities of counterfactual conditionals analogous to our earlier theory of the probabilities of indicatives. Note in passing, by the way, that if the *only* situation in which the counterfactual differed significantly from the corresponding indicative should prove to be that in which their common consequent was known to be false, then we would have an explanation as to why the counterfactual, regarded as a species logically distinct from the indicative, should be thought to entail its antecedent's falsity. This would be because the only situation in which the counterfactual could be affirmed but not the indicative would be one in which its antecedent was highly improbable. We will shortly see that things are more complicated, however.

As a preliminary to formulating a hypothesis which would account for substituting the counterfactual for the indicative, consider how this sort of substitution normally accompanies the making of a *Modus Tollens* inference. In the canary example, after seeing that the bird is blue and not yellow and substituting the counterfactual for "if that bird is a canary it will be yellow", the first speaker would be apt to conclude "that bird is not a canary." In fact, crude logical analysis might represent the man as having made a *Modus Tollens* inference from an indicative conditional premise, thus:

> If that bird is a canary it will be yellow. It is not yellow, but blue. Therefore, it is not a canary.

The foregoing would, however, seriously *mis*represent the actual reasoning by suggesting that a proposition which was actually given up before the conclusion was arrived at (the indicative conditional) was a premise, or ground, or reason for arriving at that conclusion.[1] It is more plausible to describe the man as having made a *Modus Tollens* inference with a counterfactual conditional premise instead:

> That bird is not yellow, but blue. If it were a canary it would be yellow. Therefore, it is not a canary.

Here at least both premises are propositions actually accepted at the time the conclusion is arrived at, though, granted the logical difference between the counterfactual and the indicative, we have a new problem of logical analysis because we cannot apply tests of soundness appropriate to inferences involving indicative conditionals to ones involving counterfactuals. Note, by the way, that by far the more common mood for conditional premises of real life *Modus Tollens* inferences (which are the simplest of *Reductio ad Absurdum* arguments) is the subjunctive, and therefore orthodox logic makes doubly questionable assumptions in treating them as material conditionals for the purpose of determining soundness.

We will next argue that in analyzing the foregoing reasoning it would be just as wrong to regard it simply as a *Modus Tollens* inference with a counterfactual premise as it would be to regard it as an indicative *Modus Tollens* inference. We must take into account the fact that the reasoner began by believing an indicative conditional, and then he acquired information (that the conditional's consequent was false) which resulted in two things: (1) making the original conditional improbable, though the counterfactual either remained or became probable, and (2) making the conclusion "that bird is not a canary" probable. Both of these are *probability changes*, even if only the second is something we feel happy in calling an 'inference'. Nevertheless, probability theory explains why the indicative should become improbable in the circumstances described, and we may ask whether it can also explain why the conclusion should become probable. Leaving aside for the moment the significance of the counterfactual in the reasoning, we may ask: granted that the indicative conditional was originally highly probable, and that its consequent was then established as false, *should* its antecedent thereupon *become* highly improbable, so that its negation can be affirmed? The Bayesian theory of probability change[2] shows that the answer to the foregoing question is a qualified 'yes'.

For the purpose of applying Bayesian theory, let us symbolize "that bird is a canary" and "it is yellow" by "C" and "Y", respectively. We are interested in two sets of probabilities: *prior probabilities* which apply to propositions *before* the new evidence (that the bird is not yellow, symbolized "$-Y$") is acquired, and *posterior probabilities* which apply after its acquisition. Let prior and posterior probabilities be represented by the probability functions p_0 and p_1, respectively. We can center attention on the two 'hypotheses', $-C$ and C (that the bird is not a canary and that it is a canary), and their *relative probabilities* before and after acquiring the new evidence, as given by the prior and posterior *probability ratios*, $p_0(-C)/p_0(C)$ and $p_1(-C)/p_1(C)$. Assuming that the reasoner in our example was not sure *a priori* that the bird was not a canary, the prior probability ratio $p_0(-C)/p_0(C)$ would not have been very high. If he inferred *a posteriori* that the bird was not a canary, then the posterior probability ratio $p_1(-C)/p_1(C)$ should have been high.

The following version of Bayes' Theorem relates the posterior and prior probability ratios in the example:[3]

$$(1) \qquad \frac{p_1(-C)}{p_1(C)} = \frac{p_0(-C)}{p_0(C)} \times \frac{p(-Y \text{ given } -C)}{p(-Y \text{ given } C)}.$$

The two probabilities $p(-Y \text{ given } -C)$ and $p(-Y \text{ given } C)$ are ordinarily called simply 'conditional probabilities' in probability texts, though we shall here call them *inverse conditional probabilities* to distinguish them from closely related conditional probabilities with which they might otherwise be confused. The inverse conditional probabilities are conditional probabilities of the new evidence, $-Y$, given the first hypothesis, $-C$, and given the second hypothesis, C, and in this example they necessarily equal the *prior* conditional probabilities, $p_0(-Y \& -C)/p_0(-C)$ and $p_0(-Y \& C)/p_0(C)$, respectively. What Equation (1), which is an instance of what will be called the *inverse probable inference formula*, tells us is that the posterior hypothesis probability ratio equals the prior hypothesis probability ratio multiplied by the new evidence inverse conditional probability ratio. For the posterior probability ratio to be high, then, the product of the two probability ratios on the right of Equation (1) must be high.

What we know from our description of the canary example is that prior to observing the bird's color the indicative conditional "if C then Y" was probable, hence that $p_0(Y \text{ given } C)$ was close to 1. This entails that $p_0(-Y \text{ given } C)$, which equals the inverse probability $p(-Y \text{ given } C)$ in the denominator in Equation (1), must be close to 0. That a factor in the denominator on the right of Equation (1) is close to 0 is almost enough to guarantee that the entire fraction must have a high value, which would in turn entail that the posterior probability ratio, $p_1(-C)/p_1(C)$, should be high and that $-C$ could be affirmed *a posteriori*. In fact, this inference is warranted except in two cases which are themselves of considerable significance. The two cases in which $p_1(-C)/p_1(C)$ is not high even though $p_0(Y$ given $C)$ was high and $-Y$ was then learned are: (1) the numerator inverse probability, $p(-Y$ given $-C)$, is just as low as the denominator inverse probability, and (2) the prior hypothesis probability ratio, $p_0(-C)/p_0(C)$, was itself close to 0. Either of these is a real possibiliy, and in those circumstances it is not rational to make the *Modus Tollens* inference. Case (1) is that in which, prior to observing the bird's color, it would have been rational to affirm not only "if that bird is a canary it will be yellow", but also "if that bird is not a canary it will be yellow" (the bird will be yellow, whether not it is a canary – perhaps we are in a region where all birds are yellow). In such circumstances it would obviously be irrational for a reasoner seeing a blue bird to conclude that it must not be a canary, in spite of having originally affirmed "if that bird is a canary it will be yellow." Case (2) is analogous, except that here the reasoner is certain *a priori* that the bird must be a canary, but only regards it as probable that if it is a canary it will be yellow. Under the circumstances, perceiving it to be blue will not cause the reasoner to conclude that the bird is not a canary.

The upshot of the foregoing is that though it is normally rational to infer $-C$ upon learning $-Y$, having previously affirmed 'if C then Y', there are exceptional circumstances in which this inference is not valid. What is striking about these exceptional circumstances is that they are ones in which the new information *contradicts* prior beliefs. In one case the reasoner believes that the bird will be yellow, whether or not it is a canary, and then learns something contradictory – that the bird is *not* yellow. In the other case the man believes that it is a canary and if it is a canary it will be yellow, and then he learns it is not yellow. We will see later (Section 9) that, contrary to the standard logical maxim that anything follows from a contradiction, the 'inconsistent premise' case is *almost always* an irrational *exception* to otherwise generally valid rules of 'sequential inference', where probability changes are considered explicitly. Thus, our sequential Modus Tollens *process* is rational, excepting only in the special case where the new information is inconsistent with prior beliefs, and we will see that this is an exception to almost all rules of valid inference.

According to the foregoing, the probability of $-C$ after $-Y$ is learned should depend solely on the two prior probability ratios on the right of Equation (1), and this should make one wonder what rôle could have been played by the *counterfactual* in arriving at the final conclusion of the *Modus Tollens* inference. Let us hypothesize the following as perhaps the simplest way of accounting for the counterfactual: the counterfactual plays *no* essential rôle in the *original* speaker's reasoning, but it in some way *communicates* the fact that prior to observing the bird's color, the corresponding indicative could have been (perhaps was) affirmed. Note that thus interpreted, the counterfactual in the present example is likened to a certain extent to an indirect discourse subjunctive. Whatever justifies the posterior affirmation of the counterfactual is then exactly the same as what did or might have justified the prior affirmation of the indicative, so the counterfactual can be regarded as a kind of *epistemic past tense*, expressing not what *was* the case at a prior time, but what *could have been affirmed* at the prior time. A somewhat more precise version of the 'epistemic past' hypothesis is that the probability appropriately associated with the counterfactual *a posteriori* is equal to that of the corresponding indicative conditional *a priori* – posterior counterfactual probabilities are prior indicative probabilities.

The above 'prior conditional probability hypothesis' is the one whose consequences will concern us in much of what follows, even though, as noted, it will ultimately turn out to be tenable only in limited generality. Before turning to detailed applications, there are two bits of evidence for the hypothesis which can be cited immediately. One is the already obvious fact that to the extent that the hypothesis is true we are able to account theoretically for the difference between the indicative and counterfactual conditionals, and to explain why counterfactuals are often substituted for indicatives when new information is learned. After new evidence is acquired, the indicative's probability is a posterior conditional probability which may be low *because* this new evidence was acquired, while the counterfactual's probability is a prior conditional probability which may be high because prior to acquiring the evidence the indicative conditional was probable. The second bit of evidence is that it is intuitively appropriate to use the subjunctive-counterfactual in *describing* the inverse conditional probabilities which enter into standard textbook applications of Bayesian inference. It is worth giving an example.

Consider an 'observer' who sees before him an urn, which he knows to be one of two outwardly identical urns of which one was chosen by flipping a fair coin to set before him, and which, to emphasize the analogy with the reasoning about the canary, we will call urns C and $-C$.[4] The observer also knows that both urns contain mixtures of yellow and blue balls differing only in color, and that urn C contains 99% yellow and 1% blue balls, while urn $-C$ contains 20% yellow and 80% blue balls. Armed with this information the observer now draws one ball at random from the urn in front of him, which proves to be blue, and his problem then becomes that of determining the probability which should be estimated *a posteriori* that the urn before him is urn $-C$. The information given determines directly the probability ratios entering into the right side of the inverse inference formula (1), with $p_0(-C)/p_0(C)$ equaling 1 (hypotheses equally likely *a priori*) and $p(-Y$ given $-C)$ and $p(-Y$ given $C)$ being .80 and .01, respectively (inverse-prior conditional probabilities being equal to corresponding proportions). According to Equation (1), $p_1(-C)/p_1(C)$ should then equal 80, hence *a posteriori* it is eighty times as likely that the urn in front of the man is $-C$ than that it is C. The point for us, though, is that a very natural way of describing an inverse probability such as $p(-Y$ given $C)$ in this problem is as

> the probability that a yellow ball would not have been drawn if the urn were urn C

which is of the form of a probability of a counterfactual conditional. Thus, the counterfactual is appropriate not only in informal reasoning such as that in the canary example, but also in describing the probabilities which enter the highly structured inferences typical of textbook examples of Bayesian reasoning.[5]

The following sections consider a variety of applications of the prior conditional probability hypothesis, before we encounter its difficulties.

2. COUNTERFACTUALS AND EXPLANATIONS

We get an inference involving something like explanation by modifying our canary example, and supposing that instead of seeing the bird to be blue after affirming the indicative "if that bird is a canary it will be yellow", the two observers perceive it to be *yellow* when it flies into the sunlight.

This is an observation which would tend to *confirm* the hypothesis that the bird is a canary, and the inverse inference formula can be applied to determine precisely what the posterior probability ratio of the hypotheses $-C$ and C should be as a function of their prior probability ratio, and of the inverse conditional probabilities of the new evidence (here Y instead of $-Y$) given the two hypotheses:

$$(2) \qquad \frac{p_1(-C)}{p_1(C)} = \frac{p_0(-C)}{p_0(C)} \times \frac{p(Y \text{ given } -C)}{p(Y \text{ given } C)}.$$

In this case the denominator inverse probability, $p(Y \text{ given } C)$, is close to 1 rather than 0, and so assuming that the numerator probability $p(Y \text{ given } -C)$ (the prior probability of the bird's being yellow, given that it is not a canary) is not high, it is clear that observing the bird to be yellow should decrease the probability of the bird's not being a canary and increase that of its being a canary. Explanation enters the picture here because being a canary would explain the bird's coloration, and Equation (2) gives precise expression to the common observations that possible explanations of a phenomenon must be hypotheses which would either make the phenomenon probable or at least make it more probable than would be the case *a priori*, and that establishing something which a hypothesis explains tends to confirm the hypothesis. It should be stressed that our mathematical formulation involves both prior and posterior probabilities, since this suggests that, while it is commonly argued that a general theory of explanation must involve probabilities, no adequate theory can be given in terms of probabilities *simpliciter*, ignoring distinctions of kind.

The inverse conditional probabilities entering into Equation (2) are still plausibly interpreted as the probabilities of counterfactuals which might be affirmed after observing the bird's color. Leaving aside explicit probabilities one might argue:

> That bird is likely to be a canary because it is yellow, for, if it *were* a canary it *would be* yellow.

This is an instance of a general pattern of 'explanatory inference' where it is argued that such and such an explanation is *likely*, because, if it were the case then such and such observed facts would be the case.[6] What is striking about the counterfactuals occurring in such reasoning is that they are neither equivalent to the corresponding indicative conditionals, nor do they in any sense imply the falsity or improbability of their antecedents. A person observing a bird to be yellow and affirming "if that bird were a canary it *would be* yellow" certainly does not thereby intimate that the bird is not a canary, and just as obviously the counterfactual would have a very different logical force from the wholly uninformative indicative "if that bird is a canary then it is yellow", which might be uttered under the circumstances.

Of course, merely noting the roles played by counterfactuals and prior conditional probabilities in certain kinds of inferences related to explanations does not constitute an analysis of *explanation*, and does not purport to throw light on such interesting problems as defining the connection between explanation and prediction, and explaining what is unsatisfactory about *ad hoc* explanations. We would conjecture, nevertheless, that satisfactory solutions to these problems must take into account the connections between explanations, counterfactuals, and prior probabilities. Our primary concern here, though, is with counterfactuals *per se*, and in this case as in similar applications to be noted in succeeding sections, we must leave the detailed development of the application as unfinished business.

3. LOGICAL ISOMORPHISM OF COUNTERFACTUAL AND INDICATIVE

Assuming that the probabilities of both indicative and counterfactual conditionals are representable by conditional probability functions, we would expect the two kinds of conditionals to satisfy the same logical laws. In particular, for inference patterns like the Hypothetical Syllogism which have exceptions in the indicative, we would expect parallel exceptions in the subjunctive, and where the indicative schema is universally probabilistically sound we would expect the same to hold of the corresponding counterfactual schema. These expectations are partially confirmed, but there are puzzles which lead to further interesting considerations.

As confirmation of our predicted 'logical isomorphism' of counterfactual and indicative, it is to be noted that exceptions to such generally accepted indicative schemata as the Hypothetical Syllogism and Contraposition transform into exceptions to the corresponding counterfactual schemata simply by being 'put into the epistemic past', just as the epistemic past interpretation of the counterfactual would predict. Recall the counter-instance to the Hypothetical Syllogism described in Section I.3 which involves two candidates for a public office, Jones and Smith, where Smith is the incumbent who has announced his intention of retiring to private life in the event of his defeat. Before the election it was possible to affirm the indicative conditionals "If Jones wins then Smith will retire" and "If Smith dies before the election then Jones will win", but it would be absurd to 'deduce' "If Smith dies before the election then he will retire after it." After the election, supposing Smith actually was the winner, all of these indicative conditionals would transform to the subjunctive, to yield the two acceptable premises "If Jones had won then Smith would have retired" and "If Smith had died before the election then Jones would have won", though the counterfactual 'conclusion', "If Smith had died before the election then he would have retired" would be just as absurd as in the indicative. Similarly, a counterinstance to the Contraposition pattern which was described in Section I.3 transforms to the equally absurd counterfactual inference with the premise "If it had rained yesterday there would not have been a terrific cloudburst" and conclusion "If there had been a terrific cloudburst yesterday it would not have rained."

Our epistemic past interpretation would predict that there should be no exceptions to the counterfactual transforms of such universally sound indicative patterns as the Restricted Hypothetical Syllogism, and we have not been able to construct any, although we must anticipate the likelihood of their existence in view of the limited tenability of the epistemic past interpretation. There are, however, two more immediate difficulties with the isomorphism hypothesis which will concern us in the next two sections. One has to do with the ambiguity of the counterfactual, which will be taken up in Section IV.5, and the other has to do with the fact that the isomorphism hypothesis apparently breaks down in application to inference schemata involving both factual and conditional propositions such as *Modus Ponens*. This is the topic of the following section.

4. A POSSIBLE NONCONDITIONAL COUNTERFACTUAL

The remarks in this section will be more speculative than those in previous sections, and they are made principally in the hope that some readers may find them suggestive for further work. We noted that it is an apparent limitation on our isomorphism hypothesis that there seem to be no counterfactual transforms of inferences involving both indicative conditional and factual propositions such as the *Modus Ponens* inference:

> Jones will arrive by eight p.m. If he arrives by eight then we will dine at 8:30. Therefore, we will dine at 8:30.

The problem is that while there is a counterfactual conditional corresponding to "If Jones arrives by eight then we will dine at 8:30" (namely "If Jones had arrived by eight, we would have dined by 8:30"), we don't know what the counterfactuals corresponding to the two factual propositions involved would be. Question: is there a form of English expression which is appropriately described as a 'nonconditional counterfactual'? Such expressions should stand logically to ordinary factual statements as indicative conditionals do to counterfactual conditionals, and, in particular they should fit the isomorphism hypothesis. Furthermore, assuming the epistemic past interpretation of the counterfactual, we should find that the probabilities of nonconditional counterfactuals should be prior nonconditional probabilities, and, most importantly, we should sometimes find nonconditional counterfactuals arising 'by substitution', when new information comes to hand rendering a previously probable factual proposition improbable *a posteriori*.

The 'substitution for the factual' property predicted of nonconditional counterfactuals gives us a clue. Imagine the following situation. Smith is giving a party at which Jones is to be the guest of honor, and Jones is expected to arrive by eight p.m. Prior to eight o'clock it is reasonable to affirm the factual proposition "Jones will arrive by eight p.m." Now suppose, however, that eight p.m. arrives but Jones doesn't, so that it is no longer reasonable to affirm "Jones arrived by eight p.m." (note that mere passage of time requires substitution of the factual past). On the other hand, what would probably be affirmed is "Jones *should have* arrived by eight p.m." It is at least *prima facie* plausible to regard the latter claim as communicating the fact that the corresponding factual statement could have been made at a prior time, and in fact as resting on exactly the same grounds as existed earlier for the factual proposition.[7] This would be in effect to give an epistemic past interpretation to "Jones should have arrived by eight p.m.", which in turn suggests the appropriateness of describing this statement as a nonconditional counterfactual. Granted this, it is plausible to take the inference

> Jones should have arrived by eight p.m. If he had arrived by eight we would have dined by 8:30. Therefore, we should have dined by 8:30.

as the counterfactual transform of the indicative *Modus Ponens*.

The counterfactual *Modus Ponens* has some intuitive plausibility, which confirms the isomorphism hypothesis, but obviously a broader survey is required. This matter has as yet been insufficiently studied, but the following example brings to light a difficulty both with the isomorphism hypothesis and with the epistemic past interpretation on which it is based. By isomorphism, the counterfactual inference

> If that bird were a canary it would be yellow. Therefore, it should not be the case that it is both a canary and not yellow.

should be rational, which it seems to be intuitively. However, here we are inclined to interpret the "should not be the case" in the conclusion as an inessential variant of "is not the case", since it seems rational to infer from the counterfactual premise the indicative conclusion "it is not the case that that bird is both a canary and not yellow." Indeed if the stronger indicative inference were sometimes not rational then the counterfactual conditional should sometimes be consistent with the affirmation of its antecedent coupled with the denial of its consequent, the inconsistency of which has seemed to many to be the one solid 'datum' concerning counterfactuals in what is otherwise a sea of uncertainty. The problem is that it not only does not follow from our epistemic past interpretation of "if *A* were the case then *B* would be" that this counterfactual should be inconsistent with "*A*, but not *B*", but this would actually be inconsistent with the interpretation.

Consider one of the exceptional cases in which it would not be rational to infer "that bird is not a canary" upon perceiving the bird to be blue, not yellow, in spite of having previously affirmed the indicative "if that bird is a canary it will be yellow." This is the case in which prior to observing the bird's color the reasoner was sure that the bird *was* a canary, and somewhat less sure of the indicative conditional. In the circumstances, upon seeing the bird to be blue, the reasoner would be apt to conclude "that bird is a canary, but it is not yellow." But it seems intuitively very implausible that he would affirm the counterfactual "if that bird were a canary it would be yellow" (affirmation of which would contradict the contradictoriness of "if A were the case then B would be" with "A, but not B"), in spite of the fact that by the epistemic past interpretation its probability *should* be high enough to justify affirmation (because prior to observing the bird's color, the indicative was probable enough to be affirmed). Generalizing, it would seem that in those exceptional cases where the *Modus Tollens* inference is irrational, reasoners do *not* affirm the counterfactual after giving up the indicative. If this 'disaffirmation' were itself a matter of probability (as against, say, being something dictated by helpfulness considerations), then we should have to say: (1) high prior conditional probability was at best a necessary but not a sufficient condition for the acceptability of the counterfactual; (2) the counterfactual *is* always inconsistent with the affirmation of its antecedent and denial of its consequent; and (3) counterfactual *Modus Tollens* inferences of the form

Not B. If A were the case then B would be. Therefore, not A.

were always rational.

That high prior probability may be only a necessary and not a sufficient condition for affirmability of the counterfactual may prove ultimately to be the case (Skyrms [52] appears to suggest this), but there is another possibility. What the reasoner would be apt to say after seeing the bird's color in the case just described is "if that bird is a canary then it should be yellow" (or perhaps even "if that bird should be a canary then it ought to be yellow"). And, granted that these are variants of the counterfactual, he would still be affirming a counterfactual conditional in conformity with the epistemic past interpretation. Thus, broadening the characterization of the subjunctive-counterfactual may allow us to save the epistemic past interpretation, though at the price of considering possibly logically non-equivalent counterfactuals. Again this is a matter requiring further study, but since we will encounter a far more serious problem with the epistemic past interpretation in Section 8, we shall not consider it further here.

We conclude this section by commenting briefly on possible relations between our nonconditional counterfactual "should" and the 'practical' or 'deontic'[8] reading which is the obvious one in examples like:

He should have replied pawn to King four.

or

No pets should be inside the store.

Observe that both sentences *can* have the epistemic interpretation (as against the more common 'valuational' one), and it is not unreasonable to ask whether the grammatical identy of form of many epistemic "should" statements with practical "should" statements reflects common logical properties. Put another way, it is interesting to ask how far Deontic Logic (the logic of the practical "should") is just a special case of a generalized logic of "should" (or "ought"). Though the question can scarcely be more than raised here, we will argue that at least one well known logical puzzle supposedly peculiar to Deontic Logic really arises with the epistemic "should" as well, and can therefore be regarded as a problem of the general logic of "should". This is the Good Samaritan Paradox.[9]

The logic of the paradox is made evident in the following version:

It ought to be the case that the beaten and robbed man is helped. Therefore, it ought to be the case that the man was beaten and robbed.

The conclusion follows from the premise assuming the commonly accepted 'inheritance principal': "X ought to be the case" entails "Y ought to be the case" if X entails Y. But precisely this principal fails in application to the epistemic "ought" as well, as the following example shows. Imagine a man seeing for the first time in years a boy who had been small for his age, but who has now grown to the astonishing height of six and a half feet. Pointing him out to a friend, the man might say "It ought to be the case that six and half foot boy is under six feet tall", which, according to the inheritance principal, should entail the absurd conclusion "It ought to be the case that that boy is both over and under six feet tall." This is not to say that the proper resolutions of 'paradoxical' failures of inheritance principals will be the same for both readings of "should" and "ought", but at least the analogies suggest that it may be fruitful to examine inheritance principals in a general setting, rather than just in deontic contexts. The following section, among other things, suggests an explanation for inheritance principal failures.

5. AMBIGUITY AND SCOPE

It seems to be widely recognized that counterfactuals are often ambiguous, and in this section we will discuss some of the implications of a possible explanation of this as arising in part from the nonspecificity of the "prior" in the prior probabilities which we have hypothesized as representing counterfactuals. Consider the following illustration (originally described in [5]). A party has been given and we are interested in the question of whether a particular man, Jones, attended it. Initially we know three things: (1) Jones did *not* see another man, Brown, on the evening of the party, (2) Brown does not like to be at parties where Jones is present and avoids them where possible, and (3) when not partying Jones and Brown get along very well, and often meet at a favorite bar. It is possible to argue as follows that this information *confirms* the hypothesis that Jones was at the party:

> If Jones *had* been at the party, Brown would very likely not have been, so Jones wouldn't have seen him. If Jones *had not* been at the party there is a very good chance that he would have seen Brown at the bar they both frequent. So Jones would have been less likely to have seen Brown if he had gone to the party than if he had not. Hence, since he didn't see Brown, he probably went to the party.

(this informal argument is supported if the implicit probabilities are made explicit, and the reasoning is analyzed as an inverse probable inference). Note that in the circumstances we affirm the counterfactual "If Jones had been at the party he wouldn't have seen Brown (because Brown wouldn't have been there)." Suppose now, though, that we learn that Brown *was* at the party. This would lead us to conclude that Jones was *not* at the party, arguing by a counterfactual *Modus Tollens* inference

> Jones didn't see Brown. If Jones had been at the party he would have seen Brown, because Brown was at the party. Therefore, Jones wasn't at the party.

Again probabilistic analysis confirms the soundness of this reasoning, but the point here is that now we affirm the counterfactual "If Jones had been at the party he *would* have seen Brown" (because Brown was there) which is the contrary of the earlier counterfactual. We may ask why in the circumstances we didn't continue to affirm the original counterfactual "If Jones had been at the party he wouldn't have seen Brown" (because if Jones had been at the party Brown wouldn't have been, so Jones wouldn't have seen him).

Rather than argue that one of the two counterfactuals above must be right and the other wrong *because* they are formal contraries, it seems more appropriate to say that the words used to express them are systematically ambiguous, and when they are disambiguated (a process which might involve making implicit probabilities explicit) they do not conflict. One counterfactual, "If Jones had been at the party he would not have seen Brown", corresponds to an indicative which could have been affirmed prior to learning either that Jones did not see Brown on the evening in question, or that Brown was at the party. The formal contrary corresponds to an indicative which might have been affirmed if we had first learned that Brown was at the party, and then subsequently learned that Jones did not see Brown that evening. Note, by the way, that this latter reading has the counterfactual corresponding to an indicative which could have been affirmed in *hypothetical* prior circumstances, rather than in actual ones. The necessity of broadening "prior" to include not only indicative conditionals and the probabilities which might have been assessed on actual occasions but also ones which could have been assessed on hypothetical ones will be discussed further Section 7. For the present, though, we are concerned with the mere fact of ambiguity, in particular as that ambiguity is reflected in ambiguities of the *scopes* of counterfactuals.

In Section I.6 we defined the *scope* (of antecedent restrictability) of an accepted indicative conditional to be the class of all propositions which when conjoined with the conditional's antecedent do not render it unacceptable. Applying the scope concept to material conditionals, we also noted that one way of characterizing the difference between material and indicative conditionals is to say that while material conditionals have *universal* scope (all propositions), indicative conditionals only have universal scope if they are perfectly certain, though they always include the *known world* (all propositions accepted as certainties) in their scopes. *Scope* also generalizes at least roughly to counterfactuals, so that, for instance, the proposition that the observed bird should be *wild* would fall into the scope of "If that bird were a canary it would be yellow" (as affirmed in the circumstances earlier described), since the speaker would presumably also be willing to affirm "if that bird were a wild canary it would be yellow", but the proposition that the bird should be blue would not fall into the scope because the speaker would not affirm "if that bird were a blue canary it would be yellow." This example also illustrates an important difference between indicative and counterfactual conditionals: that while indicatives' scopes include the known world, counterfactuals' scopes usually do not include all of that. In the canary example the person affirming "if that bird were a canary it would be yellow" would not affirm "if that bird were a blue canary it would be yellow", in spite of being perfectly sure that the bird was blue. In fact, at least in the case where posterior probabilities arise from prior probabilities by acquisition of new 'evidence', the scopes of the counterfactuals whose probabilities equal prior probabilities will not include the new evidence unless that can be expressed as a proposition which was already accepted *a priori*. Conversely, in the special 'limiting case' where the counterfactual's scope does include the known world, posterior probabilities must equal prior probabilities, and therefore the counterfactual and indicative will not differ in probability (all of this assuming the prior conditional probability representation, of course).

It is to be expected that ambiguities about priors will have their counterparts in ambiguities of scope in counterfactuals. Thus, one way to characterize the difference between the intended meanings of the counterfactuals "if Jones had been at the party he would have seen Brown" and "if Jones had been at the party he would not have seen Brown" in our earlier example is to say that the former is meant to include the known fact that Brown was at the party in its scope, while the latter is not intended this way. Similarly, to take the famous example of Goodman's [23] "if this penny had been in my pocket on VE day it would have been silver", allegedly *not* affirmable in spite of the postulated fact that all coins in my pocket on VE day were silver, it is possible to give this counterfactual an *acceptable* interpretation in which the fact that all coins in my pocket on VE day were silver *is* part of the counterfactual's scope, while the fact that the coin in question is a penny is not. In fact, such a reading would be the most natural one in a situation in which I am concerned with the question of whether the penny *was* in my pocket on VE day, where I might reason:

> This coin is a penny and not silver. If it had been in my pocket on VE day it would have been silver. Therefore, it was not in my pocket on VE day.

Recognizing the possible scope ambiguities of counterfactuals only leads, of course, to a new problem of trying to give the rules for disambiguation in particular contexts. This is something which requires detailed study, and we will only hazard the following concerning such rules. It is probable that in the case of *particular* counterfactuals (as against, say, counterfactuals asserting what would be the case if such and such a *general law* were not the case), the scope includes all known or strongly believed generalities, together with at least all items of particular information known about the individuals involved which are independent of and/or 'reasonably predate' the events spoken of. Thus, even in the case where Brown's being at the party is excluded from the scope of "If Jones had been at the party he wouldn't have seen Brown", the counterfactual's scope will include such generalities as that two persons at the same party can be expected to see one another, plus such particulars about Jones as that he is the man who lives at such and such a place, has such and such an appearance, and in general is "the man we know him to be."

Granted the foregoing rough rule, we can explain several counterfactual phenomena. That accepted laws "support counterfactuals" while fortuitous general truths often do not is explained by the fact that general laws normally belong to the scopes of particular counterfactuals but fortuitous general truths (e.g. that the coins in my pocket on VE day were all silver) often don't. That it is very difficult to construct future tense subjunctive-counterfactuals which differ significantly from their corresponding indicatives is explained on the assumption that counterfactuals' scopes include known information reasonably predating the events spoken of, which will include all known information for events sufficiently far into the future (recall that if a counterfactual's scope includes all the 'known world' then it will not differ in probability from the corresponding indicative).[10]

Finally, such 'paradoxes' as failures of inheritance principals and puzzles concerning 'counteridenticals' (see Goodman [23]) are, we would suggest, resolved if we simply notice that facts about individuals which are made use of in *referring* to them are often *not* part of the scopes of counterfactuals involving referring expressions. For instance, the fact that a coin is a penny, which is made use of in referring to it as "this penny" is not part of the scope of the *acceptable* reading of "if this penny had been in my pocket on VE day it would have been silver" previously noted. Similarly, the fact that a boy is six and a half feet tall is not part of the scope of the non-conditional counterfactual "it ought not to be the case that that six and a half foot boy is six and a half feet tall", considered in Section 4. And, that counteridenticals of the form "if x had been y then S would have been the case" normally include facts known about y while excluding much known about x from their scopes explains why this counterfactual is not necessarily incompatible with "if y had been x then S would not have been the case."

6. TRUTH-CONDITIONALITY AND DEFINABILITY; CONNECTIONS WITH DISPOSITIONALS

Putting aside for now problems arising from the ambiguity of the counterfactual, we may ask whether the counterfactual can be in some way 'redduced' to the factual and/or the indicative conditional, and whether it is truth-conditional. There are persuasive *prima facie* arguments that neither can be the case, and this in turn raises questions about the possibility of defining *dispositional* concepts in counterfactual terms, which is the way many have thought they should be analyzed.

Consider truth-conditionality first, or, more exactly, the question of whether the probabilities of counterfactuals can equal the probabilities of their being true. The argument that the latter cannot be the case is that at least in the case of future counterfactuals, they are equivalent (in probability) to their corresponding indicatives, and since the indicatives are not truth-conditional the counterfactuals cannot be either. It is true that we should wish to reexamine the basic assumptions of our original triviality argument of Section I.2 as they apply to counterfactual rather than indicative conditionals (especially the 'structure of the space of possible probability functions' assumption), but it would certainly be odd if what held for indicatives – non truth-conditionality – did not hold for counterfactuals which reduce to indicatives in special cases.

The question of reducibility is more complicated. The simplest kind of reduction is elimination by substitution of definitional equivalents, and there is a fairly strong argument that the counterfactual cannot be *defined* in terms just of factual or indicative conditional constructions. Granted the non truth-conditionality of the counterfactual we would not expect a definition to be a truth-conditional equivalence, but we might hope to establish a *probabilistic equivalence* of the same kind as that which defines the probability of the indicative conditional as a function of the probabilities of its antecedent and of the conjunction of its antecedent and consequent. Assuming that the probability of "if A were the case then B would be" is correctly represented as a prior conditional probability, $p_0(A \Rightarrow B)$, we would have to show that this probability could in some way be represented as a function of the probabilities of factual or indicative conditional propositions, which we have assumed to be representable by *posterior* probabilities – i.e., to define the counterfactual in terms of the factual and/or indicative conditional, we would have to define prior probabilities as functions of posterior probabilities. But it is very doubtful that this can be done. For, suppose that posterior probabilities arise from prior probabilities as a result of learning 'new evidence', E, and consider how the prior probability of E itself, $p_0(E)$, might be defined in terms of posterior probabilities. All posterior probabilities which might arise from learning E would be the same as those which would have arisen if E had been an *a priori* certainty (i.e., if $p_0(E)$ had equaled 1), and therefore it would not be possible to infer from posterior probabilities alone that $p_0(E)$ had any value other than 1.

Even assuming the impossibility of definitional reduction, we might hope to avoid the counterfactual in serious scientific contexts by some more complex procedure, say of 'paraphrasing away' in context. In fact, it seems quite plausible that such a procedure should be possible in view of our suggestion in Chapter IV, Section 1 that the counterfactual plays no *essential* rôle in leading reasoners such as the original speaker in our canary example to conclusions of what are oversimply represented as counterfactual *Modus Tollens* inferences. If this should be the case in general then to the extent that science is ultimately concerned with factual or at best indicative conditional conclusions, the counterfactual would be shown to be inessential. The following section, which is concerned with the use of the counterfactual to express what could be affirmed in *hypothetical* past circumstances rather than actual ones, makes this questionable however. Before turning to that, though, we conclude this section with some comments on connections between dispositionals and counterfactuals.

Whatever ones stand is on the issue of the *realism* of propositions involving dispositional terms, there can be no question that in ordinary practice such propositions as "*x* was water-soluble at time *t*" are treated as *though they* were factual for the purposes of logical and probabilistic analysis. Furthermore, it is not hard to see that even treating dispositional propositions as though they were factual is inconsistent with representing them as equivalent to conditionals, counterfactual or indicative, since we have argued in Chapter 1, Section 8 that such a representation would preclude attaching any probabilities to compounds such as the conjunction "both *x* and *y* were water-soluble at time *t*", and it is obvious that we do attach probabilities to these compounds. What we want to suggest here is that in fact the connection between dispositionals and counterfactuals is more complicated than that of definitional equivalence. The relation is closer akin to a probabilistic version of a *reduction sentence*, which usually simplifies to probabilistic equivalence, but does not always do so.

Consider the connection between

$$S = x \text{ was water-soluble at time } t$$

and the counterfactual

$$C = \text{if } x \text{ had been immersed in water at time } t \text{ it would have} \\ \text{dissolved.}$$

Our strong intuitive feeling that the two propositions are equivalent is what gives the commonly assumed definability of dispositionals in terms of counterfactuals its plausibility, yet there are circumstances in which the two are not equivalent. Suppose we think of the particular *x* in question that it was *not* water-soluble at time *t* and not immersed in water at that time, but that if it *had been* water-soluble at that time it would have been put into water to dissolve. Under the circumstances *S* would be almost certainly false, but *C* would be quite probable (at least in one reading) since if *x* had been immersed in water at the time this would have been because it would have been soluble.

What the foregoing suggests is equating the counterfactual C not with the factual S, but rather with a second counterfactual which has S as its consequent:

S' = if x had been immersed in water at time t then it would have been water-soluble at that time.

This gets us around the general objection to equating conditionals with nonconditional propositions, and can be seen on further analysis to accord very well with the way in which dispositional properties actually enter into probabilistic formulas. Furthermore, we have an explanation of sorts as to why the counterfactual C is commonly thought to be equivalent to the dispositional proposition S. This is because ordinarily we think immersion in water is independent of solubility (this is an instance of the general principal that carrying out defining tests for properties should not affect the properties tested for), and where independence can be assumed then C and S' are equal in probability, and hence C and S are too.

Further exploration of the connection between dispositionals and counterfactuals is obviously required, and in particular of the implications of the prior-posterior probability distinction, which we have ignored above in speaking of probabilistic equivalences among C, S, and S'. This is a matter which will be returned to briefly in Section 8, where it will be seen to be connected with a fundamental problem for the prior probability representation of counterfactuals. In spite of this difficulty, though, the foregoing should make it very plausible that whatever the connection is between counterfactuals and dispositionals, it is not one of truth-conditional or probabilistic identity. The two do stand in interesting logical relations, but the dispositional is more properly represented as factual than as conditional in form.

7. GENERALIZING TO A HYPOTHETICAL EPISTEMIC PAST INTERPRETATION

This and the next section discuss the need to generalize the epistemic past, prior probability interpretation of the counterfactual, the present section proposing a generalization which stays within the conditional probability framework, while the following section will give reasons for doubting that even this generalization is sufficient to cover many important uses of the counterfactual. We noted in Section IV.5 that one of the readings of the counterfactual "if Jones had been at the party he would have seen Brown" identifies this with an indicative which might have been affirmed not on an actual prior occasion, but rather with one affirmable on a hypothetical prior occasion in which the reasoner imagines that he learned first that Brown was not at a party, and that then Jones did not see Brown on the evening of the party (in fact, he learned these items of information in the reverse order). Obviously it will be necessary to allow identification of counterfactuals with indicatives affirmable in other than actual past circumstances if we are to account not only for the Jones-Brown example, but for such typical historical counterfactuals as "if Napoleon had been kept under stricter guard on Elba he would not have escaped, and the Battle of Waterloo would never have taken place." It is extremely implausible that anyone would ever have been in the actual position of affirming the indicative corresponding to this counterfactual, but it is not hard to describe hypothetical circumstances in which someone might do so. For instance, a person might *know* of Napoleon only that he was initially kept under rather loose guard on Elba, but that he *might* have subsequently escaped and been involved in a battle at Waterloo. Not only might the indicative conditional be affirmed here, but the person might then transform it to the subjunctive and make a counterfactual *Modus Tollens* inference upon being informed that Napoleon did escape and the Battle of Waterloo really happened.

Generalizing to the hypothetical epistemic past is also consistent with the representation of counterfactual probabilities as 'prior' conditional probabilities, since examination of applications of inverse probable inference in statistics shows that what are called 'prior probabilities' in many applications are really hypothetically prior rather than literally prior. Consider again the urn and ball-drawing example described at the end of IV.1. As originally described, the 'observer' was supposed to know *a priori* (i.e., before drawing a ball out of the urn in front of him and observing its color) that the urn before him was chosen at random between urns C and $-C$, and that the proportions of yellow balls in the two urns were .99 and .20, respectively. Under the circumstances the 'prior' unconditional probabilities, $p_0(C)$ and $p_0(-C)$, were both .5, and were both equal to what were the posterior probabilities of these hypotheses before the ball was drawn from the urn. The same holds of the prior conditional probabilities, $p(-Y$ given $C)$ and $p(-Y$ given $-C)$, entering into the problem. However, it clearly makes no difference to the problem that the items of *a priori* information were represented as having been learned *before* the 'sample' was drawn, and even if the items had been learned in reverse order it would still have been proper to represent $p_0(C)=p_0(-C)=.5$ as the 'prior probabilities' of these hypotheses, in spite of the fact that in the circumstances they would not equal what had at any actual prior time been posterior probabilities. Analogously, it would have made no difference to the reasoning in our original canary example if the reasoner had learned last that canaries are yellow, having previously learned that the bird seen was not yellow but blue. Here his affirmation of the counterfactual "if that bird were a canary it would be yellow" *a posteriori* would not express what had been previously been expressed by the corresponding indicative in actual prior circumstances, but rather what would have been expressed with the indicative in the hypothetical situation where he first knew the facts of canary coloration, before he had observed the bird to be blue.

Though it maybe somewhat fanciful to describe it thus, the foregoing suggests that hypothetical epistemic past counterfactuals are used to 'reorder epistemic history', and represent items of present knowledge as having been acquired in some other order than they actually were. Furthermore, this reordering of epistemic history may serve a purpose in reasoning, since knowing what conclusion would have been arrived at if presently known items had been acquired in some order other than the actual one is also informative about conclusions which are justified given the actual order of acquisition. Thus, suppose the reasoner in the canary example had learned the facts of canary coloration after observing the color of the bird (which might have actually been the case with his auditor). He might have made the reordering explicit in reasoning thus:

> I know that bird is blue and not yellow, and I now learn that canaries are yellow. If I had learned the latter first, I could have affirmed that if that bird were a canary it would be yellow, and then I could have concluded that the bird was not a canary upon observing that it was not yellow. Therefore, since it makes no difference in which order I learned my facts,

> I can conclude in my present situation that the bird is not a canary.

A number of things may be noted about the above reasoning, and in particular about the counterfactual

> If I had learned the latter first (that canaries are yellow), I could have affirmed that if that bird were a canary it would be yellow.

which occurs in it. It is plausible to describe this as the *explicit epistemic expansion* of the embedded counterfactual "if that bird were a canary it would be yellow", since it makes it explicit that the latter expresses what could have been expressed with the corresponding indicative if the reasoner had known initially that canaries are yellow (note that the "were... would..." of the embedded counterfactual now becomes that of indirect discourse, which is suggestive concerning the connection between the 'counterfactual' subjunctive and the indirect discourse subjunctive). Further, the expansion makes explicit in part what is inside of the scope of the embedded counterfactual, namely the fact that canaries are yellow, and the context makes it clear that the bird's actual coloration is outside of the scope. Finally, the 'reordering of epistemic history' use of the counterfactual makes it questionable that the counterfactual has no essential rôle to play in reasoning in which it enters. So long as its use is merely to communicate to others reasons for arriving at conclusions already reached, the counterfactual may be inessential (except to get others to reach those conclusions), but it is at least possible that the counterfactual is essential in leading reasoners to conclusions which, but for 'hypothetical reasoning', are only reached if information is acquired in the 'right' order.

Whatever ones conclusions are about the dispensability of the counterfactual, it is clear that the hypothetical epistemic past is a broad generalization of our earlier actual epistemic past interpretation of the counterfactual. Nonetheless this interpretation still fits the 'prior' conditional probability interpretation, provided that is generalized in a way which is consistent with actual practice in applying the theory of inverse probable (Bayesian) inference. The following section, however, makes it extremely implausible that even this broadened interpretation of the counterfactual can accomodate many of its significant uses.

8. A COUNTEREXAMPLE

Imagine the following situation. We have just entered a room and are standing in front of a metal box with two buttons marked 'A' and 'B' and a light, which is off at the moment, on its front panel. Concerning the light we know the following. It may go on in one minute, and whether it does or not depends on what combinations of buttons A and B, if either, have been pushed a short while before, prior to our entering the room. If exactly one of the two buttons has been pushed then the light will go on, but if either both buttons or neither button has been pushed then it will stay off. We think it highly unlikely that either button has been pushed, but if either or both were pushed then they were pushed independently, the chances of A's having been pushed being 1 in a thousand, while the chances of B's having been pushed is a very remote 1 in a million. In the circumstances we think there is only a very small chance of 1,000,999 in one billion (about 1 in a thousand) that the light will go on, but a high probability of 999 in a thousand that *if B was pushed, the light will go on*.

Now suppose that to our surprise the light does go on, and consider what we would infer in consequence. Leaving out numerical probabilities for the moment, we would no doubt conclude that the light probably lit because A was pushed and B wasn't, and not because B was pushed and A wasn't. Therefore, since A was probably the button pushed, *if B had been pushed the light wouldn't have gone on*, for then both buttons would have been pushed. The point here is that the counterfactual would be affirmed *a posteriori* in spite of the fact that the corresponding indicative was very improbable *a priori*, because its contrary "if B was pushed then the light will go on" had a probability of .999 *a priori*.

The informal reasoning above is supported if numerical probabilities are considered, as least so far as concerns the factual and indicative conditional propositions involved. Letting 'A' and 'B' abbreviate 'A was pushed" and "B was pushed", respectively, and "L" abbreviate "the light will (did) go on", and representing posterior and prior probabilities (before and after the light's going on) by p_0 and p_1, respectively, the inverse inference formula tells us:

$$(3) \qquad \frac{p_1(B)}{p_1(A)} = \frac{p_0(B)}{p_0(A)} \times \frac{p(L \text{ given } B)}{p(L \text{ given } A)}.$$

The prior unconditional probability ratio, $p_0(B)/p_0(A)$, is directly given as $(1/1,000,000)/(1/1,000) = .001$. The two inverse-prior conditional probabilities can be computed as follows:

$$
\begin{aligned}
(4) \qquad p(L \text{ given } B) &= p_0(B \Rightarrow L) \\
&= p_0(B \Rightarrow A)p_0(B \text{ \& } A \Rightarrow L) \\
&\quad + p_0(B \Rightarrow - A)p_0(B \text{ \& } - A \Rightarrow L) \\
&= p_0(B \Rightarrow A)\cdot 0 + p_0(B \Rightarrow - A)\cdot 1 \\
&= p_0(B \Rightarrow - A) \\
&= p_0(- A) = .999,
\end{aligned}
$$

and by parity of reasoning,

$$
(5) \qquad p(L \text{ given } A) = p_0(- B) = .999999.
$$

Substituting these values into Equation (3) gives:

$$
(6) \qquad \frac{p_1(B)}{p_1(A)} = \frac{p_0(B)}{p_0(A)} \times \frac{p_0(-A)}{p_0(-B)} = \frac{.000001}{.001} \times \frac{.999}{.999999} = \frac{999}{999999}.
$$

Note in particular that the prior conditional probability $p_0(B \Rightarrow L)$ *was* high (.999), and that it was this high prior probability which was substituted into the inverse inference formula (3) in order to compute the correct relative posterior probabilities of B and A.

Not only cannot the counterfactual "if B had been pushed the light would not have gone on" be identified with the corresponding indicative prior to the light's going on, but it is even dubious that this counterfactual's probability can be assumed to satisfy the usual laws of conditional probability. Symbolizing as before, but letting p be any arbitrary conditional probability function which *might* represent counterfactuals' probabilities in the present situation, we would have:

$$
\begin{aligned}
(7) \qquad p(B \Rightarrow - L) &= p(B \Rightarrow A)p(B \text{ \& } A \Rightarrow - L) + p(B \Rightarrow - A) \\
&\quad \times p(B \text{ \& } - A \Rightarrow - L),
\end{aligned}
$$

and since $p(B \text{ \& } A \Rightarrow - L)$ would obviously be 1 while $p(B \text{ \& } - A \Rightarrow - L)$ would be 0, we would have

$$
p(B \Rightarrow - L) = p(B \Rightarrow A).
$$

The right hand counterfactual probability would be the probability that if B had been pushed then A would also have been pushed, and this is most plausibly taken to be the *prior* probability of A's being pushed, .001. On the other hand, we have already argued that $p(B \Rightarrow -L)$ equals the posterior probability of A's having been pushed, which is .999. If our identification of $p(B \Rightarrow A)$ above is correct, this would imply that Equation (7), which is a pure law of conditional probability, cannot hold for the counterfactuals involved. And, if present counterfactual probabilities do not satisfy the standard laws of conditional probabilities, it follows *a fortiori* that these counterfactuals cannot even be given a hypothetical epistemic past interpretation.

There is an important similarity between aspects of our button and light example and certain kinds of reasoning about dispositional propositions. We can regard the pushing of button A as putting the electrical circuit inside the box into a dispositional state in which the pushing of B results in the light's not going on, where the mere fact of the light's actually going on can constitute evidence, positive or negative, that A was pushed and the circuit was in this state. Something similar can arise in reasoning about, say, whether a given object x (which *a priori* might or might not have been dissolved at some prior time t) was or was not soluble at time t. Learning that x was not dissolved at t might under certain circumstances be evidence that x was not soluble at t, and that if x had been immersed in water at that time it would not have dissolved. It is this fact which causes difficulties not so much with relating dispositionals to conditional probabilities as outlined in the last section, but with identifying those probabilities in some systematic way with what would be posterior probabilities in either actual or hypothetical prior states.

A rather simple minded generalization of our prior conditional probability representation which would accomodate counterfactuals entering into the button and light example (as well as certain dispositional examples) is as follows. Restrict attention to the counterfactual "if B had been pushed the light would not have gone on", whose probability is assumed to be given by $p(B \Rightarrow -L)$. Generalizing, we may syppose there are mutually exclusive and exhaustive states $S_1, \ldots, S_n$ which are causally independent of B, and which together with B causally determine $-L$. In this case, the probability of the counterfactual is plausibly given by:

$$(8) \qquad p(B \Rightarrow -L) = \sum_{i=1}^{n} p_1(S_i) \, p_0(B \, \& \, S_i \Rightarrow -L).$$

In the particular case under consideration, the two causally independent states are just A and $-A$, and these play the role of dispositional states.

The foregoing 'two factor model' of counterfactual probabilities is admittedly *ad hoc*, and we will only make the following brief remarks concerning it. What it does is to represent counterfactuals as dependent on: (1) particular states, S_i, which may be dispositional in character, and (2) general causal or at least nomological connections relating the antecedent of the counterfactual together with the states S_i to the counterfactual's consequent. Most important, whereas the counterfactual's probability depends on the *prior* probabilities associated with the causal laws, it depends on the *posterior* probabilities of the states. It is the mixture of the prior and posterior probabilities in this combination which accounts for the counterfactual's not satisfying the usual laws of conditional probability, whereas the literal prior probability of the corresponding indicative conditional is given when the posterior state probabilities are replaced by prior probabilities, and the posterior indicative probability results when the causal law probabilities are replaced by posterior conditional probabilities. If there are no states (independent of B) which need to be considered, then the counterfactual's probability will be a prior conditional probability, and so the two factor model reduces to the epistemic past model in this case.

It is an interesting sidelight on the two factor model that the requirement that B be *causally* independent of the states S_i cannot be replaced by the requirement that these factors be *statistically* independent. Imagine the button and light example modified in the following way. We suppose that first a spinner with one million equal divisions is spun to determine whether B is pushed (it is pushed only if a "1" comes up). Then, depending on what the upshot of the first spinning has been, one of two identical spinners with a thousand divisions is spun to determine whether A is to be pushed (A is pushed only if "1" comes up). Here all of the probabilities are as they were originally described, but if the spinner which is spun to determine whether A is pushed depends on the outcome of the first spinner's spin, then A and B are not causally independent, and in fact we wouldn't affirm the same counterfactuals as in the case where they are causally independent. Observing the light to go on, we would indeed conclude that in all likelihood A was pushed and B was not, but we would probably not affirm "if B had been pushed the light would not have gone on", since if B had been pushed a different spinner would have been used to determine whether A should be pushed, and under the circumstances A would probably not have been pushed and the light would have gone on.

The *ad hoc* two factor model clearly requires far more searching investigation than has been considered here, but we will conclude this section by mentioning what seems to be the chief obstacle in the further logical analysis of the counterfactual. This is that, with the exception of counterfactual *Modus Tollens* inference and its generalizations to confirmation-explanation inferences and *Reductio ad Absurdum* arguments, it is very difficult to isolate systematic inference patterns involving counterfactuals but issuing in factual conclusions. This is the case in particular with the counterfactual "if B had been pushed the light wouldn't have gone on", which, though we may feel strongly that it is 'the right thing to say' in the example, does not seem to be an 'item of information' which might contribute to arriving at further factual knowledge. Lacking any factual and indirectly practical consequences of these counterfactuals, they take on the empty speculative character of 'Monday morning quarterbacking' wherein we are at a loss to say just what better and worse opinions are because in fact nothing serious depends on them.[11] The question we should ask, then, is whether there *are* further inference patterns besides Counterfactual *Modus Tollens* and its generalizations in which counterfactual premises contribute (even if indirectly) to factual conclusions, the rationality of which would give us a basis for assessing the counterfactuals involved. This is the major open question with which we must conclude our discussion of the counterfactual.

9. INFERENCE AS PROBABILITY CHANGE; COMMENTS ON WHAT CAN BE INFERRED FROM CONTRADICTORY PREMISES

Whatever one thinks of the epistemic past hypothesis about counterfactuals, our analysis of *Modus Tollens* in IV.1 puts that normally unquestioned pattern in a new light where 'arriving at the conclusion' is viewed as a probability change which results when new information is acquired. Moreover, when so interpreted the 'inference process' no longer appears to be universally sound. In this and the next section we will inquire more generally into the implications of this change of viewpoint.

Consider *two stage inference processes* of the following type: A reasoner initially accepts *prior premises* $\mathscr{A}_1, ..., \mathscr{A}_n$, then learns a *new premise* $\mathscr{B}$, and arrives in consequence at a *conclusion* $\mathscr{C}$. This section will consider two stage processes in which the prior premises are all either factual or simple conditional propositions, while the new information and the conclusion are both factual. We want to know what are the circumstances in which the conclusion $\mathscr{C}$ will be probable *a posteriori*, and for the purpose of determining this we will let p_0 and p_1 represent prior and posterior probabilities, respectively; i.e., probabilities attaching to propositions before and after the new premise is learned. Granted that the prior premises were accepted *a priori*, the prior probabilities $p_0(\mathscr{A}_1), ..., p_0(\mathscr{A}_n)$ should all be high. That $\mathscr{B}$ is a new premise means that $p_1(\mathscr{B})$ should be high, and in fact we will assume that posterior probabilities arise from prior probabilities by conditionalizing on $\mathscr{B}$: i.e., for *any* factual proposition $\mathscr{C}$,

$$(9) \qquad p_1(\mathscr{C}) = p_0(\mathscr{B} \Rightarrow \mathscr{C}).$$

If $\mathscr{C}$ is the new premise $\mathscr{B}$ itself, clearly $p_1(\mathscr{C})$ will be 1, and so we are assuming that the new premise is an *a posteriori* certainty. This is an idealization which will be reconsidered in IV.10.

The two stage process described above will be universally sound if it is impossible for the prior probabilities $p_0(\mathscr{A}_1), ..., p_0(\mathscr{A}_n)$ all to be high while the posterior probability of the conclusion, $p_1(\mathscr{C}) = p_0(\mathscr{B} \Rightarrow \mathscr{C})$ is low. Clearly a necessary condition for this is that the *corresponding one stage process* with premises $\mathscr{A}_1, ..., \mathscr{A}_n$ and $\mathscr{B}$, and conclusion $\mathscr{C}$ to be universally sound in the sense of chapters I and II. However, this condition is not sufficient, as *Modus Tollens* with prior premise $A \Rightarrow B$, new premise $-B$, and conclusion $-A$ illustrates. The necessary condition for the universal soundness of the two stage process is that the one stage process with premises $A \Rightarrow B$ and $-B$ and conclusion $-A$ should be sound, which is the case. However, the necessary and sufficient condition for the universal soundness of the two stage process is that it should be impossible for $p_0(A \Rightarrow B)$ to be high while $p_1(-A) = p_0(-B \Rightarrow -A)$ is low, which is clearly not the case since this essentially is the Contraposition inference pattern, which we know is not universally sound. Of course, this only confirms what we found already in IV.1; namely that two stage *Modus Tollens* is not universally sound. On the other hand two stage *Modus Ponens* with prior premise $A \Rightarrow B$, new premise A, and conclusion B is universally sound, since here $p_1(B) = p_0(A \Rightarrow B)$, so B will be as probable *a posteriori* as the prior premise was *a priori* (however, we will see in IV.10 that things change when the order of premises is reversed).[12]

The technique just described for determining universal soundness can be applied to two stage processes not involving conditionals at all. To illustrate, consider the process with prior premise $A \vee B$, new premise $-A$, and conclusion B. This process is universally sound if and only if it is not possible for $p_0(A \vee B)$ to be high while $p_1(B) = p_0(-A \Rightarrow B)$ is low. But we saw in Chapter 1, Section 3 that $p_0(A \vee B)$ can be arbitrarily close to 1 while $p_0(-A \Rightarrow B)$ is zero, hence this two stage process is not universally sound in spite of the fact that the corresponding one stage process is sound. A counterexample to the inference of $-A \Rightarrow B$ from $A \vee B$ described in I.3 also transforms into a counterexample to the present two stage process. We might now believe "either it will rain or it will snow in Berkeley next year" and then learn from a highly reliable soothsayer "it will not rain in Berkeley next year", in which case it would not be rational to conclude "it will snow in Berkeley next year" – *because* it was not rational to accept "if it doesn't rain then it will snow in Berkeley next year."

The last example illustrates a significant generalization. This is that if an essential prior premise is *factual* (the two stage process with that premise deleted would not be universally sound), then a two stage process cannot be universally sound unless the new premise (and conclusion) is not really new because it in fact follows from the prior premises. This follows from Theorem 3.7, according to which if $\mathscr{A}_1$ is an essential factual premise to the inference of $\mathscr{B} \Rightarrow \mathscr{C}$ from $\mathscr{A}_1, ..., \mathscr{A}_n$, then the inference can only be universally sound if the inference with the same premises and conclusion $\mathscr{B} \& \mathscr{C}$ is also universally sound. It begins to look as though the conditional is the essential 'tie which binds past and present' when prior knowledge and new information are combined to arrive at new conclusions.

From the point of view of real life applications partial soundness is probably more important than universal soundness, and we will next make a brief remark on this very complicated subject. Assume that the one stage process corresponding to the two stage process with prior premises $\mathscr{A}_1, ..., A_n$, new premise $\mathscr{B}$, and conclusion $\mathscr{C}$ *is* universally sound. Then there are two partial soundness circumstances for the two stage process which are significant. One is that in which the new premise belongs to the scopes of all of the prior premises. In this case learning the new premise will not result in having to give up any prior premise, so all prior premises *plus* the new premises will be accepted *a posteriori* and therefore $\mathscr{C}$ can be concluded in virtue of the universal soundness of the one stage inference of $\mathscr{C}$ from $\mathscr{A}_1, ..., \mathscr{A}_n$ and $\mathscr{B}$. Note that this explains the universal soundness of two stage *Modus Ponens*, because here the new information, A, always belongs to the scope of the prior premise $A \Rightarrow B$ (anything entailed by the antecedent of an accepted conditional belongs to the scope of that conditional). The second partial soundness case is that in which the *denial* of the new premise was not itself accepted *a priori*. This partial soundness condition reduces to the 'belonging to the prior scopes' condition when prior premises are factual (because in that case only *a priori* very improbable premises can fall outside their scopes), but can differ from the latter when prior premises are conditional, as *Modus Tollens* illustrates. In the *Modus Tollens* case the new premise $-B$ *always* falls outside the scope of the prior premise $A \Rightarrow B$, since $A \& -B \Rightarrow B$ is never acceptable, and yet the inference will still be sound so long as the contrary of the new premise was not accepted *a priori*. Observe that it is where a new premise falls outside the scope of a prior premise yet the inference is still rational that we are led to employ the counterfactual to 'explain' the inference. Note too that this never happens in the case of inferences with factual prior premises, which suggests that nonconditional counterfactuals may have no rôle to play in arriving at factual conclusions.

Very roughly, what we have shown is that two stage processes corresponding to universally sound one stage processes are sound except possibly when the new premise *contradicts* prior beliefs both in that: (1) acceptance of the new premise entails giving up a prior premise, and (2) before the new premise was learned, its contradictory was accepted. This is of course a very limited and crude rule, but we would still argue that it constitutes an advance over the traditional maxim "anything follows from a contradiction" as a theory of what it is rational to believe when confronted with conflicting data and conclusions. One thing the rule shows is that an adequate theory of 'conflict reasoning' must make distinctions ignored in traditional theory, e.g., between premises accepted at the same time and those learned 'sequentially' (and, possibly more importantly, between *actual* and *hypothetical* contradiction as the latter might be considered in *Reductio ad Absurdum* arguments). More importantly, though, probabilistic analysis of *Modus Tollens* in the exceptional 'conflict' case shows that an adequate theory of that case cannot be given in truth conditional terms alone, ignoring probabilities. For instance, in the canary example in which the reasoner originally believes both "if that bird is a canary it will be yellow" and "if that bird is not a canary it will be yellow" and then sees that the bird is blue, Equation (1) shows that what it is rational to conclude depends critically not just on the fact that the two conditionals were accepted *a priori*, but on *how probable* they were. If the first had been much more certain than the second, for example, it would still have been rational to conclude that the bird was not a canary. This illustrates the general point that what is inferrable in the face of conflict is not just a matter of what is accepted and what is not, but rather of degrees of certainty.

Of course, the foregoing hardly does more than point out there *is* a problem so far as concerns giving an adequate theory of inference in the presence of conflict, and that it is unlikely that real progress can be made with the problem within the frame of the orthodox truth-conditional conceptual scheme. We would conjecture, though, that orthodox *probabilities* cannot make much headway with the problem either, so long as those are unable to reflect probability changes resulting from *deductive* discoveries (as against changes resulting from learning new premises). Hintikka's paper [32] is a pioneering effort at developing a more adequate theory, but consideration of this would carry us beyond the scope of the present work.

10. EXTENSIONS INVOLVING APPROXIMATE CONDITIONALIZATION

We would like to extend our theory of sequential inference processes so as to be able to apply it to processes with new premises and conclusions of *conditional* form, and also to ones of more than two stages. Unfortunately even the simplest of these extensions – to processes with conditional conclusions – requires us to give up the idealization that new premises are *a posteriori* certainties, if a realistic theory is to be developed. To see this, consider the process with no prior premises, new premise B, and conclusion $A \Rightarrow B$. The corresponding one stage process is the inference of $A \Rightarrow B$ from B, which is clearly not universally sound, yet if the new premise B is assumed to be certain *a posteriori*, then $p_1(A \Rightarrow B)$ must also be certain, from which it would follow that the two stage process was universally sound. Obviously we cannot continue to assume that new premises are certain, and we will here sketch aspects of a 'model' of probability change resulting from learning somewhat uncertain new premises which hopefully offers a more realistic account of the phenomena which concern us. As it happens when uncertainties are allowed in new premises, almost none of the processes we are interested in prove to be universally sound, and our primary interest then turns to questions of partial soundness. This topic is very complicated, however, and we will content ourselves here with merely formulating the partial soundness problem, and will defer detailed discussion to future publication.

A first approximation model of uncertain conditionalization which we will consider is appropriately called a *question-response* model, according to which, when a reasoner is *represented* as having learned a new premise, $\mathscr{B}$, what really happens is that he has asked the question "is $\mathscr{B}$ the case?", and a respondent has replied that $\mathscr{B}$ is the case. The basic assumption of the model is that what the reasoner has really learned as a certainty is that the question has been asked and the response given, and that posterior probabilities arise from prior probabilities by conditionalizing on these certainties. Formally, if $Q(\mathscr{B}) = Q$ expresses the fact that "is $\mathscr{B}$ the case?" was asked and $R(\mathscr{B}) = R$ expresses the fact that the respondent has replied that $\mathscr{B}$ is the case, then we assume that the posterior probability of any factual conclusion, $\mathscr{C}$, will be given by $p_1(\mathscr{C}) = p_0(Q \ \& \ R \Rightarrow \mathscr{C})$.[13,14]

Before applying the QR model to inferences, consider how our postulated posterior probabilities arising by *QR conditionalization* (by conditionalizing on $Q(\mathscr{B}) \ \& \ R(\mathscr{B})$) relate to what may be called their *$\mathscr{B}$-approximations*; namely the probabilities $p_0(\mathscr{B} \Rightarrow \mathscr{C})$ which would be posterior probabilities if $\mathscr{B}$ were the certain new premise. The following inequality of pure probability theory provides some information:

$$(10) \qquad |p_0(Q \ \& \ R \Rightarrow \mathscr{C}) - p_0(Q \ \& \ \mathscr{B} \Rightarrow \mathscr{C})| \leqslant u_0(Q \ \& \ R \Rightarrow \mathscr{B}) \\ + u_0(Q \ \& \ \mathscr{B} \Rightarrow R),$$

where u_0 is the uncertainty (1 minus probability) function corresponding to p_0. The left hand term, $p_0(Q \ \& \ R \Rightarrow \mathscr{C})$, is of course the QR conditionalization which we are postulating to equal $p_1(\mathscr{C})$, the posterior probability of $\mathscr{C}$. Making three key assumptions, which will also be central to the theory of inference, we can also say something about the values of the other three terms in (10). It is plausible that merely asking the question "is $\mathscr{B}$ the case?" is probabilistically *independent* of both $\mathscr{B}$ and $\mathscr{C}$, and if that is the case then $p_0(Q \,\&\, \mathscr{B} \Rightarrow \mathscr{C})$ will equal $p_0(\mathscr{B} \Rightarrow \mathscr{C})$, which is the $\mathscr{B}$-approximation of the posterior probability of $\mathscr{C}$. Assuming independence (the *independence assumption*), then, the left side of (10) is the absolute value of the difference between the postulated 'true' posterior probability of $\mathscr{C}$ and its $\mathscr{B}$-approximation.

$u_0(Q \,\&\, R \Rightarrow \mathscr{B})$ is the *a priori* uncertainty that, if the question is asked and the respondent replies that $\mathscr{B}$ is the case, then $\mathscr{B}$ is in fact the case. Assuming that the respondent is *truthful* this uncertainty will be small, and we will call the assumption that $Q \,\&\, R \Rightarrow \mathscr{B}$ has small uncertainty (hence high probability) the *truthfulness premise*. $u_0(Q \,\&\, \mathscr{B} \Rightarrow R)$ is the uncertainty that if the respondent is asked "is $\mathscr{B}$ the case?" and $\mathscr{B}$ is the case, then he will reply that $\mathscr{B}$ is the case. Assuming that the respondent is *informed* and *helpful* this uncertainty will be low. We will call the assumption that $Q \,\&\, \mathscr{B} \Rightarrow R$ is highly probable the *informedness and helpfulness premise*. Combining the independence assumption and the truthfulness and informedness and helpfulness premises it follows that the difference between true posterior probabilities and their $\mathscr{B}$-approximations must be small.[15]

Now return to the two stage inference process with prior premises $\mathscr{A}_1, ..., \mathscr{A}_n$, new premise $\mathscr{B}$, and conclusion $\mathscr{C}$, where we will begin by assuming as before that both $\mathscr{B}$ and $\mathscr{C}$ are factual. If we now suppose that not $\mathscr{B}$ but $Q(\mathscr{B}) \,\&\, R(\mathscr{B})$ was what was really learned as a certainty, then the above process is appropriately called the $\mathscr{B}$-*approximation process*. In general, the QR *elaboration* of this process will be the process with the same prior premises and conclusions as in the original process, but with new premise $Q \,\&\, R$ instead of $\mathscr{B}$. If we assume independence, truthfulness, and informedness and helpfulness, however, we can add these explicitly to the elaboration, and define the *special QR elaboration* process as follows. The prior premises will include the formulas $\mathscr{A}_1(Q), ..., \mathscr{A}_n(Q)$ plus the truthfulness and informedness and helpfulness premises, $Q \,\&\, R \Rightarrow \mathscr{B}$ and $Q \,\&\, \mathscr{B} \Rightarrow R$, where $\mathscr{A}_i(Q)$ is the *narrowing* of $\mathscr{A}_i$ to Q which results when Q is conjoined to the antecedent of $\mathscr{A}_i$. Assuming Q is independent of each $\mathscr{A}_i$, the prior probability of $\mathscr{A}_i(Q)$ will equal that of $\mathscr{A}_i$, hence the narrowed prior premises are also affirmable *a priori*. The new premise of the special elaboration will now be Q & R, and the conclusion will be the same as that of the original $\mathscr{B}$-approximation.

Now we may ask what connection there is between the soundness of the $\mathscr{B}$-approximation process and the special QR elaboration process. So far as concerns universal soundness, the answer is simple: one process is universally sound if and only if the other is. To prove this it is sufficient to prove that the two one stage processes

$$\frac{\mathscr{A}_1, ..., \mathscr{A}_n}{\mathscr{B} \Rightarrow \mathscr{C}}$$

and

$$\frac{\mathscr{A}_1(Q), ..., \mathscr{A}_n(Q), Q \& R \Rightarrow \mathscr{B}, Q \& \mathscr{B} \Rightarrow R}{Q \& R \Rightarrow \mathscr{C}}$$

are equivalent in universal soundness. The latter follows easily from Theorem 3 of Chapter II, assuming only that Q and R are atomic formulas not occurring at all in the approximation process. The upshot is that so far as concerns universal soundness, introducing the possibility of uncertainty in new premises does not change the picture for processes with factual premises and conclusions.

Now consider the simplest generalization, where the $\mathscr{B}$-approximation process has prior premises $\mathscr{A}_1, ..., \mathscr{A}_n$, new premise $\mathscr{B}$, and *conditional* conclusion $\mathscr{C}_1 \Rightarrow \mathscr{C}_2$. As before, we can take the special QR elaboration process to be the one with prior premises $\mathscr{A}_1(Q), ..., \mathscr{A}_n(Q)$ plus $Q \& R \Rightarrow \mathscr{B}$ and $Q \& \mathscr{B} \Rightarrow R$, new premise $Q \& R$, all as before, but conditional conclusion $\mathscr{C}_1 \Rightarrow \mathscr{C}_2$. If posterior probabilities are assumed to arise from priors by conditionalizing on Q & R, then we should have:

$$p_1(\mathscr{C}_1 \Rightarrow \mathscr{C}_2) = p_0(Q \& R \& \mathscr{C}_1 \Rightarrow \mathscr{C}_2).$$

It is easily seen that if the special QR elaboration process is to be universally sound, it must be the case that the inference

$$\frac{\mathscr{A}_1(Q), ..., \mathscr{A}_n(Q), Q \& R \Rightarrow \mathscr{B}, Q \& \mathscr{B} \Rightarrow R}{Q \& R \& \mathscr{C}_1 \Rightarrow \mathscr{C}_2}$$

is universally sound. But it follows from theorems of Chapter II that this inference can only be universally sound if the simpler inference

$$\frac{\mathscr{A}_1, ..., \mathscr{A}_n, \mathscr{B}}{\mathscr{C}_1 \Rightarrow \mathscr{C}_2}$$

is universally sound. And, by Theorem 3.7, if $\mathscr{B}$ is essential to the latter inference then it can only be universally sound if the inference with the same premises and conjunctive conclusion $\mathscr{C}_1$ & $\mathscr{C}_2$ is universally sound. In other words, the special QR elaboration process with conditional conclusion $\mathscr{C}_1 \Rightarrow \mathscr{C}_2$ can only be sound if the process with the much stronger factual conclusion $\mathscr{C}_1$ & $\mathscr{C}_2$ is also universally sound (so long as the new information is essential to the conclusion), and we have no 'interesting' two stage processes with conditional conclusions which are universally sound. Of course, the foregoing should lead us to inquire into conditions of partial soundness, but this is a complicated matter, and as with other extensions of the basic theory, we must leave the problem for more detailed discussion elsewhere.

The simplest generalization of two to many stage processes is that in which a reasoner first accepts prior premises $\mathscr{A}_1, \ldots, \mathscr{A}_n$ as before, then learns a *first new* (factual) *premise* $\mathscr{B}_1$, then learns a *second new* (factual) *premise* $\mathscr{B}_2$, and then arrives at a factual conclusion $\mathscr{C}$. It is clear that so long as the new premise certainty idealization is accepted, the foregoing three stage process will appear to be equivalent so far as concerns soundness to the two stage process with prior premises $\mathscr{A}_1, \ldots, \mathscr{A}_n$, new premise the conjunction $\mathscr{B}_1$ & $\mathscr{B}_2$, and conclusion $\mathscr{C}$. In other words, essential generalization from two to more than two stages requires dropping the posterior premise certainty idealization.

The natural generalization of the QR model of uncertain new premises is to suppose that for each new premise $\mathscr{B}_i$, what is really learned when a reasoner is described as having learned $\mathscr{B}_i$ is that the question "is $\mathscr{B}_i$ the case?" has been asked, and a respondent has replied that $\mathscr{B}_i$ is the case. Symbolizing, let Q_i express the proposition that "is $\mathscr{B}_i$ the case?" has been asked, and let R_i express the proposition that this question has been answered in the affirmative. Then the special QR elaboration of the $\mathscr{B}_1$, $\mathscr{B}_2$-approximation process with prior premises $\mathscr{A}_1, \ldots, \mathscr{A}_n$, first and second new premises $\mathscr{B}_1$ and $\mathscr{B}_2$, respectively, and conclusion $\mathscr{C}$, is appropriately taken to be the process with prior premises $\mathscr{A}_1(Q_1$ & $Q_2), \ldots,$ $\mathscr{A}_n(Q_1$ & $Q_2)$ (narrowing original prior premises to Q_1 & Q_2, justified by independence assumptions), plus Q_1 & $R_1 \Rightarrow \mathscr{B}_1$ and Q_2 & $R_2 \Rightarrow \mathscr{B}_2$ (truthfulness premises) and Q_1 & $\mathscr{B}_1 \Rightarrow R_1$ and Q_2 & $\mathscr{B}_2 \Rightarrow R_2$ (informedness and helpfulness premises), first and second new premises Q_1 & R_1 and Q_2 & R_2, respectively, and conclusion $\mathscr{C}$. If it is assumed that the probability of $\mathscr{C}$ after the second new premise is learned is given by p_2, and that posterior probabilities arise from prior probabilities by conditionalizing on the conjunction of Q_1 & R_1 and Q_2 & R_2, it follows that

$$p_2(\mathscr{C}) = p_0(Q_1 \ \& \ R_1 \ \& \ Q_2 \ \& \ R_2 \Rightarrow \mathscr{C}).$$

This in turn implies that the special QR elaboration process will be universally sound if and only if the inference

$$\frac{\mathscr{A}_1(Q_1 \ \& \ Q_2), ..., \mathscr{A}_n(Q_1 \ \& \ Q_2), Q_1 \ \& \ R_1 \Rightarrow \mathscr{B}_1,}{Q_1 \ \& \ R_1 \ \& \ Q_2 \ \& \ R_2 \Rightarrow \mathscr{C}}$$
$$Q_2 \ \& \ R_2 \Rightarrow \mathscr{B}_2, Q_1 \ \& \ \mathscr{B}_1 \Rightarrow R_1, Q_2 \ \& \ \mathscr{B}_2 \Rightarrow R_2$$

is universally sound. Here again, however, it is easy to show that the complicated QR elaboration above can only be universally sound if the inference

$$\frac{\mathscr{A}_1, ..., \mathscr{A}_n, \mathscr{B}_1}{\mathscr{B}_2 \Rightarrow \mathscr{C}}$$

is universally sound. But this can only be universally sound if either $\mathscr{B}_1$ is an inessential premise, or in fact the inference to the stronger conclusion $\mathscr{B}_2$ & $\mathscr{C}$ is also universally sound: i.e., one of the two premises must be inessential.

Of course, the difficulty with three stage inferences just noted could have been foreseen. We noted in the previous section that even assuming posterior premise certainty, all essential prior premises of universally sound two stage processes had to be of conditional form. In a three stage process, all original prior premises *plus* the first new premise play the rôle of prior premises in moving from the second to the third stage, which means that if the first new premise is essential to the inference, it must itself be of conditional form. Hence, so long as we seek universal soundness but allow new premises not to be *a posteriori* certainties, we must consider new premises of conditional form. We will conclude with some very brief comments on the very difficult problem of giving an adequate theory of multi-stage inferences processes involving new premises which are conditionals.

Perhaps the most interesting application of the QR model is to provide a framework for describing the influence on beliefs of acquiring information of non-factual forms. In particular, in the case where a reasoner is represented as having learned a conditional proposition $\mathscr{B}_1 \Rightarrow \mathscr{B}_2$, we may suppose that what has really happened is that he has asked "is $\mathscr{B}_1 \Rightarrow \mathscr{B}_2$ the case?", and someone has replied in the affirmative. Of course, we want to know how the effect of learning Q & R compares with or is related to the *content* of the proposition $\mathscr{B}_1 \Rightarrow \mathscr{B}_2$. As with the QR elaboration of factual new premises, we can assume that simply asking "is $\mathscr{B}_1 \Rightarrow \mathscr{B}_2$ the case?" is independent of prior accepted propositions, and in particular for any accepted prior premise $\mathscr{A}_i$, its narrowing to $\mathscr{A}_i(Q)$ is also accepted. Likewise, there is a kind of generalization of the truthfulness premise, which is the assumption that Q & R & $\mathscr{B}_1 \Rightarrow \mathscr{B}_2$ is probable *a priori*. Assuming that posterior probabilities arise from prior probabilities by conditionalizing on Q & R, this would imply that $p_1(\mathscr{B}_1 \Rightarrow \mathscr{B}_2)$ should be high: i.e., $\mathscr{B}_1 \Rightarrow \mathscr{B}_2$ should be probable *a posteriori*, which is what we should expect upon being told $\mathscr{B}_1 \Rightarrow \mathscr{B}_2$ by a truthful person. The problem, to which we see no easy solution, is that there is no obvious analogue to the informedness and helpfulness premise, and that lacking such an analogue it is very difficult to state any universally sound rules of inference involving new premises of conditional form.

Omitting any analogue to the informedness and helpfulness premise, we might want to assume tentatively that the appropriate special QR elaboration of the process with prior premises $\mathscr{A}_1, ..., \mathscr{A}_n$, new (approximate) premise $\mathscr{B}_1 \Rightarrow \mathscr{B}_2$, and (factual) conclusion $\mathscr{C}$ was the process with prior premises $\mathscr{A}_1(Q), ..., \mathscr{A}_n(Q)$, plus Q & R & $B_1 \Rightarrow \mathscr{B}_2$, new premise Q & R, and conclusion $\mathscr{C}$. Assuming posterior probabilities arise by conditionalizing on Q & R, this process would be universally sound if and only if the one stage inference

$$\frac{\mathscr{A}_1(Q), ..., \mathscr{A}_n(Q), Q \ \& \ R \ \& \ \mathscr{B}_1 \Rightarrow \mathscr{B}_2}{Q \ \& \ R \Rightarrow \mathscr{C}}$$

were universally sound. As would be expected, a necessary condition for the universal soundness of this inference is that the inference

$$\frac{\mathscr{A}_1, ..., \mathscr{A}_n, \mathscr{B}_1 \Rightarrow \mathscr{B}_2}{\mathscr{C}}$$

should be universally sound. However, assuming that R is an atomic formula not occurring in the approximate process, this condition will be sufficient only when the conclusion follows from $\mathscr{B}_1 \Rightarrow \mathscr{B}_2$ alone.

The foregoing result, that QR elaborations of processes with conditional new premises are only universally sound if their conclusions follow from the new premises alone, depends critically on the fact that we have not included an analogue to the informedness and helpfulness premise in the suggested QR elaboration. This is a matter deserving of further comment, but before turning to that we may ask how well this result accords with real life reasoning which takes place as a result of learning information expressed in conditional form. Without undertaking a detailed survey, we can say that we have been able to find very few two stage inference processes with conditional new premises which are always rational in real life. The simplest illustration is *Modus Ponens* with the conditional premise learned *second*. Suppose a reasoner initially thinks concerning two men, Smith and Jones, that Smith probably played and Jones certainly played in a given game. Now he learns as a certainty that if Smith played then Jones did *not* play, with the result that rather than inferring "Jones did not play" by *Modus Ponens* from "Smith did play", instead he gives up his prior premise "Smith played."

The foregoing is of course just one more illustration of the fact that normally sound inference patterns can be unsound in the special case where a new premise *conflicts* with an essential prior premise in such a way that accepting the new premise entails giving up the old one. What we seek in an adequate theory of inferences processes like our *reversed Modus Ponens* process (with factual premise accepted first and conditional premise learned second) is therefore an account of the conditions under which learning conditional new premises will *not* conflict with prior premises in the above sense. We have an account of this in the factual new premise case, namely that the factual new premise must belong to the *scopes* of the essential prior premises, and we know what is required for membership in the scope of a proposition. The problem is to generalize this so as to be able to say what the conditions are for a *conditional* proposition to belong to the scope of a prior premise. One might argue that generalizing the scope concept in such a way that conditionals can belong to the scopes of propositions requires defining the probabilities of conditionals which contain conditionals in their antecedents (because we have defined a factual proposition to belong to the scope of a premise if conjoining the factual to the antecedent of the premise does not make the latter unacceptable), but we would suggest that the root of the problem lies in an analysis of the conditional *utterance,* and in particular with getting a clearer understanding of something like informedness and helpfulness 'premises' as they might apply to conditionals. Thus, though we have been able to ignore linguistic and communicational aspects of conditional propositions throughout the body of this work, it now appears that they must be taken into account if we are to understand the effect of learning conditionals as new premises. But this is as yet very much *terra incognita.*

NOTES

1 The implicit claim here, that premises of inferences should be *reasons* for arriving at conclusions, obviously takes 'premise' in a narrower sense than is common in logical theory, where *assumptions* (such as occur in *Reductio ad Absurdum* arguments) are normally called premises.

2 The Bayesian theory of probability change, an illustration of which is given at the end of this section, is a standard part of elementary probability theory, and is usually given in the first two or three chapters of texts such as Feller [19] or Uspensky [58].

3 This version of Bayes' Theorem, which generalizes to arbitrary hypotheses which may be neither mutually exclusive nor exhaustive in place of $-C$ and C, is particularly useful in its neat separation of hypothesis likelihood ratios and inverse conditional probability ratios. It is appropriate to call this case of the inverse inference formula the *probabilistic Modus Tollens formula* because it appears to give a probabilistic generalization of *Modus Tollens.* We will encounter an analogous *probabilistic Modus Ponens formula* in Section 9.

4 In fact, the present urn and ball example can be looked upon as a *stochastic model* of the inference in the canary example. Analogous stochastic models can be given for many kinds of reasoning where there is a reason to pay attention to implicit uncertainties, and they give considerable insight into the question of how these uncertainties may affect the uncertainty of the conclusion.

5 It must be conceded that the subjunctive is rarely, if ever, *used* in textbook descriptions of inverse conditional probabilities (which are commonly described as 'conditional probabilities' *simpliciter,* or in some such form as "the probability of A, assuming that B", as in Uspensky ([58], p. 61). I would hazard the following contentious conjecture concerning this. This is that probability theorists either do not conceive of, or ignore the possibility that *conditional* probabilities should be just as susceptible to change 'in the light of new evidence' as unconditional probabilities. At any rate, this would explain why 'proofs' such as those of I. J. Good [22], and Raiffa and Schlaiffer [44] that making new observations (as against refraining from observing) is always desirable (because it decreases expected entropic uncertainty and increases expected utility of the results of acting) normally go unquestioned in spite of obvious counterexamples which arise when the observer's subjective conditional probabilities are *mistaken* in the sense of Section III.7 (cf. an example appearing in my review [6]).

6 This may be an example of 'inference to the best explanation' as considered in the writings of Harmon (e.g., [28]). My attention was first drawn to such uses of the counterfactual by a nice instance in *The Hound of the Baskervilles* ([15], p. 684), where Sherlock Holmes begins an explanation with the words "if that were so, and it seems most probable,...".

[7] This 'epistemic past tense' reading of "it should have been (should be) the case that ..."
looks at least *prima facie* to be very close to Ryle's analysis of the *actual* past tense in
Concept of Mind (chapter on Memory, see also Shwayder [48]). If, as I think there is,
there is something in Ryle's view, this may show that the *actual* past is not to be
analyzed independently of the counterfactual.

[8] The identification of the deontic with the *practical* 'ought' is borrowed from
Vermazen [59], to which I am indebted for most of the little I know about Deontic
Logic.

[9] See, e.g., Vermazen (59), p. 17 or Nozick and Routley [43].

[10] There are possible exceptions to the rule that future counterfactuals are equivalent
to their corresponding indicatives, at least if the 'going to' construction is regarded as
future. Knowing for certain that *B* isn't going to play in such and such a game, one
might well affirm 'if *A* were the manager then *B* would be going to play" but deny "if *A*
is the manager then *B* is going to play". On the other hand, this may be taken as one
more bit of evidence that "is going to" is logically present and not future. In any case,
I have been unable to construct any other 'pure future' counterexamples to the thesis
that future counterfactuals are equivalent to indicatives.

[11] Perhaps a consideration of the use of counterfactuals in descriptions of fair damages
(e.g. damages equal to what an injured person would have been able to earn, if the in-
jury had not occurred) would be useful in this connection. It is interesting that this
type of counterfactual use also occurs in the rules of certain games, as in the rule pre-
scribing the penalty for *obstructing* a runner or batter-runner in baseball, where it is
stipulated that the runners shall advance to the bases they would have reached, in the
umpire's judgment, if there had been no obstruction ([9], p. 23).

[12] For this reason it is appropriate to regard Equation (7) as the probabilistic generalization of the *Modus Ponens* inference rule.

[13] This QR approximation theory is plausibly adaptable to the situation in which new
information is acquired by *observation*, where the act of asking question *Q* is replaced
by that of *making* an observation (e.g., looking to see what color some object is), and
the 'response' is replaced by the direct *result* of the observation (e.g., to learn that the
object at least *seems* to have such and such a color). The model becomes, perhaps,
philosophically suspect in this interpretation, because of its close connections with
dubious sense data epistemologies.

[14] The present QR approximation model should be contrasted with an approximate
conditionalization model proposed by Jeffrey [34], and developed in detail by Harper
[29], according to which the posterior probability, $p_1(\mathscr{C})$, arising from the acquisition
of a somewhat uncertain new premise $\mathscr{B}$ is given by

$$\alpha p_0(\mathscr{B} \Rightarrow \mathscr{C}) + (1 - \alpha)p_0(-\mathscr{B} \Rightarrow \mathscr{C}),$$

where α is an 'uncertainty parameter' close to but generally somewhat less than 1. The
Jeffrey model is *inconsistent* with the QR model in the sense that if α differs from 0 and 1
and Q and R are in the domain of definition of p_0, then the Jeffrey posterior probability
given above cannot always equal the QR posterior probability, $p_0(Q \& R \Rightarrow \mathscr{C})$ (in
particular, these probabilities cannot be equal for $\mathscr{C} = Q \& R$). The two models are
compatible in the weaker sense that, given any Jeffrey posterior probability as defined by the above weighted average over a fixed class of propositions C, it is possible
to *extend* the domain of definition of p_0 by adjoining new propositions Q and R to it
in such a way that the QR posterior probability will equal the Jeffrey posterior probability for all propositions in the original domain of p_0. If we think of Q and R as being, in

a sense, subjective 'hidden variables', which should not be part of the 'public domain' of p_0, perhaps the foregoing is enough to reconcile the two models.

[15] Equation (8), together with the interpretations just given of its four terms, usefully pinpoints what goes wrong in certain alleged counterexamples to the rule of probability change by conditionalization, such as the following striking 'paradox of three job-seekers' described in Gardner [20]. Three men, *A*, *B*, and *C*, have applied for one job with *a priori* equal chances of getting it. The management has decided who is to get the job, but hasn't yet announced its decision. Candidate *A* approaches the manager and asks whether he got the job, but is told that the decision can't be made public yet. *A* then says "if you won't tell me whether I got the job, at least tell me the name of one person besides myself who *didn't* get it." The manager relents to the extent of telling *A* that *B* didn't get the job, whereupon *A* feels somewhat better because he now thinks his chances have improved (from $\frac{1}{3}$ to $\frac{1}{2}$) for getting the job. These improved chances are those which would follow if posterior probabilities were computed by conditionalizing on the new premise $\mathscr{B} = -B$ (B didn't get the job), yet it takes little thought to see that in fact being told that *B* didn't get the job should *not* lead *A* to alter his prior estimate of his chances – because he could have foretold *a priori* that the manager would be able to tell him the name of *someone* besides himself who didn't get the job. The trouble here lies in the relation between the question (or demand) that the manager should tell *A* the name of someone besides *A* who didn't get the job, and the manager's response that *B* didn't get the job. The analogue of the informedness and helpfulness premise does not hold in this case, because it is not highly probable *a priori* that if *this* question is asked and *B* didn't get the job, then the manager will *respond* that *B* didn't get the job (if neither *B* nor *C* got the job, the manager might just as easily have replied that *C* didn't get the job). In fact, here the informedness and helpfulness uncertainty, $u_0(Q \ \& \ \mathscr{B} \Rightarrow R)$, can be as high as $\frac{1}{4}$, hence the proper QR posterior probability that *A* got the job, which in this case equals the prior probability of $\frac{1}{3}$, can differ from the $\mathscr{B}$-approximation (which is $\frac{1}{2}$) by as much as $\frac{1}{4}$, even if all other uncertainties are 0.

BIBLIOGRAPHY

[1] Adams, E. W., 'On the Logic of Conditionals', *Inquiry* **8** (1965), 166–197.

[2] Adams, E. W., 'Probability and the Logic of Conditionals', in J. Hintikka and P. Suppes (ed.), *Aspects of Inductive Logic*, North-Holland, 1966, pp. 265–316.

[3] Adams, E. W., 'Subjunctive and Indicative Conditionals', *Foundations of Language* **6** (1970), 89–94.

[4] Adams, E. W., 'The Logic of "Almost All"', *Journal of Philosophical Logic* **3** (1974), 3–17.

[5] Adams, E. W., 'Counterfactual Conditionals and Prior Probabilities', to appear in C. A. Hooker and W. Harper (eds.), *Proceedings of International Congress on the Foundations of Statistics*, D. Reidel, 1975.

[6] Adams, E. W., review of J. Hintikka and P. Suppes (eds.), *Information and Inference*, *Synthese* **25** (1972), 234–240.

[7] Adams, E. W. and Levine, H. P., 'On the Uncertainties Transmitted from Premises to Conclusions in Deductive Inferences', to appear in *Synthese*, 1975.

[8] Ayers, M., "Counterfactuals and Subjunctive Conditionals", *Mind*, 1965, 347–364.

[9] *Official Baseball Rules Revised Edition*, copyright 1969 by the Commissioner of Baseball.

[10] Carlstrom, I., 'Truth and Entailment for a Vague Quantifier', to appear in *Synthese*, 1975.

[11] Cooper, W. S., 'The Propositional Logic of Ordinary Discourse', *Inquiry* **11** (1968), 295–320.

[12] Cooper, W. S., *Logico-Linguistics*, unpublished manuscript, University of California, Berkeley, 1974.

[13] de Finetti, B., 'La prévision: ses lois logiques, ses sources subjectives', *Annales de l'Institut Henri Poincaré* **7** (1936), 1–68.

[14] Dodgson, C. (Lewis Carroll), 'A Logical Paradox', *Mind*, N.V. (1898), 436–440.

[15] Conan Doyle, Sir A., *The Hound of the Baskervilles*, in *The Complete Sherlock Holmes*, Doubleday & Co., Inc., 1930.

[16] Dummett, M., 'Truth', *Proc. Arist. Soc.* **59** (1958–59), 141–162.

[17] Ellis, B., 'Probability Logic', unpublished manuscript, 1968.

[18] Ellis, B., *Epistemological Foundations of Logic*, unpublished manuscript, La Trobe University 1971.

[19] Feller, W., *An Introduction to Probability Theory and its Applications*, 2nd edition, Wiley, 1960.

[20] Gardner, M., 'Probability Paradoxes', in M. Gardner (ed.), *The Scientific American Book of Puzzles and Diversions*, Simon and Schuster, 1959, pp. 47–54.

[21] Goguen, J. A., 'The Logic of Inexact Concepts', *Synthese* **19** (1968–69), 325–373.

[22] Good, I. J., 'On the Principle of Total Evidence', *British Journal for the Philosophy of Science* **17** (1967), 319–321.

[23] Goodman, N., *Fact, Fiction, and Forecast*, 2nd edition, The Bobbs-Merrill Co. Inc., 1965.

[24] Grice, H. P., 'Meaning', *Philosophical Review* **66** (1957), 377–388.
[25] Grice, H. P., 'Utterers' Meanings and Intentions', *Philosophical Review* **78** (1969), 147–177.
[26] Grice, H. P., *William James Lectures*, unpublished manuscript.
[27] Hanna, J., 'A New Approach to the Formation and Testing of Learning Models', *Synthese* **16** (1966), 344–380.
[28] Harmon, G., 'The Inference to the Best Explanation', *Philosophical Review* **74** (1965), 88–95.
[29] Harper, W. L. and May, S., 'Applying a Minimum Change Principle to Probability Kinematics', to appear in C. A. Hooker and W. L. Harper (eds.), *Proceedings of International Congress on the Foundations of Statistics*, D. Reidel, 1975.
[30] Henkin, L. and Montague, R., 'On the Definition of "Formal Deduction"', *Journal of Symbolic Logic* **21** (1956), 129–136.
[31] Heyting, A., *Intuitionism, an Introduction*, North-Holland, 1956.
[32] Hintikka, J., 'Surface Information and Depth Information', in J. Hintikka and P. Suppes (eds.), *Information and Inference*, D. Reidel, 1970.
[33] Jeffrey, R., 'If' (abstract), *Journal of Philosophy* **61** (1964), 702–703.
[34] Jeffrey, R., *The Logic of Decision*, McGraw-Hill, 1965.
[35] Khinchine, A. I., *Mathematical Foundations of Information Theory*, English translation by R. A. Silverman and M. D. Friedman, Dover, 1957.
[36] Kolmogorov, A. N., *Foundations of Probability*, English translation by N. Morrison, Chelsea, 1950.
[37] Krantz, D. and Luce, R. D., 'Conditional Expected Utility', *Econometrica* **39** (1971), 253–271.
[38] Krantz, D., Luce, R. D., Suppes, P., and Tversky, A., *Foundations of Measurement*, Vol. 1, Academic Press, 1971.
[39] Kyburg, H., 'Probability, Rationality, and the Rule of Detachment', in Y. Bar-Hillel (ed.), *Logic, Methodology, and Philosophy of Science*, North-Holland, 1967, pp. 301–310.
[40] Lewis, D., 'Conditional Probabilities and Probabilities of Conditionals', unpublished notes, Princeton, 1973.
[41] Lewis, D., *Counterfactuals*, Harvard University Press, 1974.
[42] Luce, R. D. and Raiffa, H., *Games and Decisions*, Wiley, 1954.
[43] Nozick, R. and Routley, R., 'Escaping the Good Samaritan Paradox', *Mind* **71** (1962), 377–382.
[44] Raiffa, H. and Schlaifer, R., *Applied Statistical Decision Theory*, Harvard Business School.
[45] Ramsey, F. P., *The Foundations of Mathematics and Other Logical Essays*, Routledge, Kegan-Paul, 1931.
[46] Ryle, G., *The Concept of Mind*, Hutchinson's University Library, 1949.
[47] Savage, L. J., *The Foundations of Statistics*, Wiley, 1954.
[48] Shwayder, D. S., 'The Temporal Order', *The Philosophical Quarterly* **10** (1960), 32–43.
[49] Shwayder, D. S., *The Stratification of Behavior*, Routledge, Kegan-Paul, 1965.
[50] Skyrms, B., 'Contraposition of the Conditional', *Philosophical Studies* **24** (1974), 1–21.
[51] Skyrms, B., 'Physical Law and the Nature of Philosophical Reduction', to appear in G. Maxwell (ed.), *Minnesota Studies in the Philosophy of Science*, Vol. 6, 1975.
[52] Skyrms, B., 'Can the Inferential Probability Conditional Survive David Lewis'

Triviality Proof?', mimeographed notes, University of Chicago, Chicago Circle, 1974.

[53] Stalnaker, R. C., 'A Theory of Conditionals', in N. Rescher (ed.), *Studies in Logical Theory*, Blackwell, 1968.

[54] Stalnaker, R. C., 'Probability and Conditionals', *Philosophy of Science* **37** (1970), 68–80.

[55] Strawson, P. F., *Introduction to Logical Theory*, Methuen & Co. Ltd., 1954.

[56] Suppes, P., 'Probabilistic Inference and the Principal of Total Evidence', in J. Hintikka and P. Suppes (eds.) *Aspects of Inductive Logic*, North-Holland, 1966, pp. 49–65.

[57] Teller, P., 'Conditionalization, Observation, and Change of Preference', to appear in C. A. Hooker and C. W. Harper (eds.), *Proceedings of International Congress on the Foundations of Statistics*, D. Reidel, 1975.

[58] Uspensky, J. V., *Introduction to Mathematical Probability*, McGraw-Hill, 1937.

[59] Vermazen, B., *The Logic of Practical 'Ought' Sentences*, unpublished manuscript, University of California, Berkeley, 1975.

[60] van Fraassen, B. C., 'Probabilities of Conditional' to appear in C. W. Hooker and W. A. Harper (eds.), *Proceedings of International Congress in the Foundations of Statistics*, D. Reidel, 1975.

[61] von Neumann, J. and Morgenstern, O., *Theory of Games and Economic Behavior*, Princeton University Press, 1953.

[62] Zadeh, L. A., 'Probability Measures of Fuzzy Sets', *Journal of Math. Analysis and Applications* **22** (1968), 421–427.

[63] Zadeh, L. A. and Bellman, R. E., 'Decision-Making in a Fuzzy Environment', *Management Science* **17** (1970), 141–164.

INDEX OF NAMES

INDEX OF SUBJECTS

SYNTHESE LIBRARY

Monographs on Epistemology, Logic, Methodology,
Philosophy of Science, Sociology of Science and of Knowledge, and on the
Mathematical Methods of Social and Behavioral Sciences

Managing Editor:

JAAKKO HINTIKKA (Academy of Finland and Stanford University)

Editors:

ROBERT S. COHEN (Boston University)
DONALD DAVIDSON (The Rockefeller University and Princeton University)
GABRIËL NUCHELMANS (University of Leyden)
WESLEY C. SALMON (University of Arizona)

1. J. M. BOCHEŃSKI, *A Precis of Mathematical Logic.* 1959, X + 100 pp.
2. P. L. GUIRAUD, *Problèmes et méthodes de la statistique linguistique.* 1960, VI + 146 pp.
3. HANS FREUDENTHAL (ed.), *The Concept and the Role of the Model in Mathematics and Natural and Social Sciences, Proceedings of a Colloquium held at Utrecht, The Netherlands, January 1960.* 1961, VI + 194 pp.
4. EVERT W. BETH, *Formal Methods. An Introduction to Symbolic Logic and the Study of Effective Operations in Arithmetic and Logic.* 1962, XIV + 170 pp.
5. B. H. KAZEMIER and D. VUYSJE (eds.), *Logic and Language. Studies dedicated to Professor Rudolf Carnap on the Occasion of his Seventieth Birthday.* 1962, VI + 256 pp.
6. MARX W. WARTOFSKY (ed.), *Proceedings of the Boston Colloquium for the Philosophy of Science, 1961-1962*, Boston Studies in the Philosophy of Science (ed. by Robert S. Cohen and Marx W. Wartofsky), Volume I. 1973, VIII + 212 pp.
7. A. A. ZINOV'EV, *Philosophical Problems of Many-Valued Logic.* 1963, XIV + 155 pp.
8. GEORGES GURVITCH, *The Spectrum of Social Time.* 1964, XXVI + 152 pp.
9. PAUL LORENZEN, *Formal Logic.* 1965, VIII + 123 pp.
10. ROBERT S. COHEN and MARX W. WARTOFSKY (eds.), *In Honor of Philipp Frank*, Boston Studies in the Philosophy of Science (ed. by Robert S. Cohen and Marx W. Wartofsky), Volume II. 1965, XXXIV + 475 pp.
11. EVERT W. BETH, *Mathematical Thought. An Introduction to the Philosophy of Mathematics.* 1965, XII + 208 pp.
12. EVERT W. BETH and JEAN PIAGET, *Mathematical Epistemology and Psychology.* 1966, XII + 326 pp.
13. GUIDO KÜNG, *Ontology and the Logistic Analysis of Language. An Enquiry into the Contemporary Views on Universals.* 1967, XI + 210 pp.

14. ROBERT S. COHEN and MARX W. WARTOFSKY (eds.), *Proceedings of the Boston Colloquium for the Philosophy of Science 1964–1966, in Memory of Norwood Russell Hanson*, Boston Studies in the Philosophy of Science (ed. by Robert S. Cohen and Marx W. Wartofsky), Volume III. 1967, XLIX + 489 pp.
15. C. D. BROAD, *Induction, Probability, and Causation. Selected Papers.* 1968, XI + 296 pp.
16. GÜNTHER PATZIG, *Aristotle's Theory of the Syllogism. A Logical-Philosophical Study of Book A of the Prior Analytics.* 1968, XVII + 215 pp.
17. NICHOLAS RESCHER, *Topics in Philosophical Logic.* 1968, XIV + 347 pp.
18. ROBERT S. COHEN and MARX W. WARTOFSKY (eds.), *Proceedings of the Boston Colloquium for the Philosophy of Science 1966–1968*, Boston Studies in the Philosophy of Science (ed. by Robert S. Cohen and Marx W. Wartofsky), Volume IV. 1969, VIII + 537 pp.
19. ROBERT S. COHEN and MARX W. WARTOFSKY (eds.), *Proceedings of the Boston Colloquium for the Philosophy of Science 1966–1968*, Boston Studies in the Philosophy of Science (ed. by Robert S. Cohen and Marx W. Wartofsky), Volume V. 1969, VIII + 482 pp.
20. J. W. DAVIS, D. J. HOCKNEY, and W. K. WILSON (eds.), *Philosophical Logic.* 1969, VIII + 277 pp.
21. D. DAVIDSON and J. HINTIKKA (eds.), *Words and Objections: Essays on the Work of W. V. Quine.* 1969, VIII + 366 pp.
22. PATRICK SUPPES, *Studies in the Methodology and Foundations of Science. Selected Papers from 1911 to 1969.* 1969, XII + 473 pp.
23. JAAKKO HINTIKKA, *Models for Modalities. Selected Essays.* 1969, IX + 220 pp.
24. NICHOLAS RESCHER *et al.* (eds.), *Essays in Honor of Carl G. Hempel. A Tribute on the Occasion of his Sixty-Fifth Birthday.* 1969, VII + 272 pp.
25. P. V. TAVANEC (ed.), *Problems of the Logic of Scientific Knowledge.* 1969, XII + 429 pp.
26. MARSHALL SWAIN (ed.), *Induction, Acceptance, and Rational Belief.* 1970, VII + 232 pp.
27. ROBERT S. COHEN and RAYMOND J. SEEGER (eds.), *Ernst Mach; Physicist and Philosopher*, Boston Studies in the Philosophy of Science (ed. by Robert S. Cohen and Marx W. Wartofsky), Volume VI. 1970, VIII + 295 pp.
28. JAAKKO HINTIKKA and PATRICK SUPPES, *Information and Inference.* 1970, X + 336 pp.
29. KAREL LAMBERT, *Philosophical Problems in Logic. Some Recent Developments.* 1970, VII + 176 pp.
30. ROLF A. EBERLE, *Nominalistic Systems.* 1970, IX + 217 pp.
31. PAUL WEINGARTNER and GERHARD ZECHA (eds.), *Induction, Physics, and Ethics, Proceedings and Discussions of the 1968 Salzburg Colloquium in the Philosophy of Science.* 1970, X + 382 pp.
32. EVERT W. BETH, *Aspects of Modern Logic.* 1970, XI + 176 pp.
33. RISTO HILPINEN (ed.), *Deontic Logic: Introductory and Systematic Readings.* 1971, VII + 182 pp.
34. JEAN-LOUIS KRIVINE, *Introduction to Axiomatic Set Theory.* 1971, VII + 98 pp.
35. JOSEPH D. SNEED, *The Logical Structure of Mathematical Physics.* 1971, XV + 311 pp.
36. CARL R. KORDIG, *The Justification of Scientific Change.* 1971, XIV + 119 pp.

37. MILIČ ČAPEK, *Bergson and Modern Physics*, Boston Studies in the Philosophy of Science (ed. by Robert S. Cohen and Marx W. Wartofsky), Volume VII, 1971, XV + 414 pp.
38. NORWOOD RUSSELL HANSON, *What I do not Believe, and other Essays* (ed. by Stephen Toulmin and Harry Woolf), 1971, XII + 390 pp.
39. ROGER C. BUCK and ROBERT S. COHEN (eds.), *PSA 1970. In Memory of Rudolf Carnap*, Boston Studies in the Philosophy of Science (ed. by Robert S. Cohen and Marx W. Wartofsky, Volume VIII. 1971, LXVI + 615 pp. Also available as a paperback.
40. DONALD DAVIDSON and GILBERT HARMAN (eds.), *Semantics of Natural Language*. 1972, X + 769 pp. Also available as a paperback.
41. YEHOSUA BAR-HILLEL (ed.), *Pragmatics of Natural Languages*. 1971, VII + 231 pp.
42. SÖREN STENLUND, *Combinators, λ-Terms and Proof Theory*. 1972, 184 pp.
43. MARTIN STRAUSS, *Modern Physics and Its Philosophy. Selected Papers in the Logic, History, and Philosophy of Science*. 1972, X + 297 pp.
44. MARIO BUNGE, *Method, Model and Matter*. 1973, VII + 196 pp.
45. MARIO BUNGE, *Philosophy of Physics*. 1973, IX + 248 pp.
46. A. A. ZINOV'EV, *Foundations of the Logical Theory of Scientific Knowledge (Complex Logic)*, Boston Studies in the Philosophy of Science (ed. by Robert S. Cohen and Marx W. Wartofsky), Volume IX. Revised and enlarged English edition with an appendix, by G. A. Smirnov, E. A. Sidorenka, A. M. Fedina, and L. A. Bobrova. 1973, XXII + 301 pp. Also available as a paperback.
47. LADISLAV TONDL, *Scientific Procedures*, Boston Studies in the Philosophy of Science (ed. by Robert S. Cohen and Marx W. Wartofsky), Volume X. 1973, XII + 268 pp. Also available as a paperback.
48. NORWOOD RUSSELL HANSON, *Constellations and Conjectures* (ed. by Willard C. Humphreys, Jr.), 1973, X + 282 pp.
49. K. J. J. HINTIKKA, J. M. E. MORAVCSIK, and P. SUPPES (eds.), *Approaches to Natural Language. Proceedings of the 1970 Stanford Workshop on Grammar and Semantics*. 1973, VIII + 526 pp. Also available as a paperback.
50. MARIO BUNGE (ed.), *Exact Philosophy – Problems, Tools, and Goals*. 1973, X + 214 pp.
51. RADU J. BOGDAN and ILKKA NIINILUOTO (eds.), *Logic, Language, and Probability*. A selection of papers contributed to Sections IV, VI, and XI of the Fourth International Congress for Logic, Methodology, and Philosophy of Science, Bucharest, September 1971. 1973, X + 323 pp.
52. GLENN PEARCE and PATRICK MAYNARD (eds.), *Conceptual Chance*. 1973, XII + 282 pp.
53. ILKKA NIINILUOTO and RAIMO TUOMELA, *Theoretical Concepts and Hypothetico-Inductive Inference*. 1973, VII + 264 pp.
54. ROLAND FRAÏSSÉ, *Course of Mathematical Logic – Volume I: Relation and Logical Formula*. 1973, XVI + 186 pp. Also available as a paperback.
55. ADOLF GRÜNBAUM, *Philosophical Problems of Space and Time*. Second, enlarged edition, Boston Studies in the Philosophy of Science (ed. by Robert S. Cohen and Marx W. Wartofsky), Volume XII. 1973, XXIII + 884 pp. Also available as a paperback.
56. PATRICK SUPPES (ed.), *Space, Time, and Geometry*. 1973, XI + 424 pp.
57. HANS KELSEN, *Essays in Legal and Moral Philosophy*, selected and introduced by Ota Weinberger. 1973, XXVIII + 300 pp.

58. R. J. SEEGER and ROBERT S. COHEN (eds.), *Philosophical Foundations of Science. Proceedings of an AAAS Program, 1969.* Boston Studies in the Philosophy of Science (ed. by Robert S. Cohen and Marx W. Wartofsky), Volume XI. 1974, X + 545 pp. Also available as a paperback.

59. ROBERT S. COHEN and MARX W. WARTOFSKY (eds.), *Logical and Epistemological Studies in Contemporary Physics,* Boston Studies in the Philosophy of Science (ed. by Robert S. Cohen and Marx W. Wartofsky), Volume XIII. 1973, VIII + 462 pp. Also available as a paperback.

60. ROBERT S. COHEN and MARX W. WARTOFSKY (eds.), *Methodological and Historical Essays in the Natural and Social Sciences. Proceedings of the Boston Colloquium for the Philosophy of Science, 1969–1972,* Boston Studies in the Philosophy of Science (ed. by Robert S. Cohen and Marx W. Wartofsky), Volume XIV. 1974, VIII + 405 pp. Also available as paperback.

61. ROBERT S. COHEN, J. J. STACHEL, and MARX W. WARTOFSKY (eds.), *For Dirk Struik. Scientific, Historical and Political Essays in Honor of Dirk J. Struik,* Boston Studies in the Philosophy of Science (ed. by Robert S. Cohen and Marx W. Wartofsky), Volume XV. 1974, XXVII + 652 pp. Also available as paperback.

62. KAZIMIERZ AJDUKIEWICZ, *Pragmatic Logic,* transl. from the Polish by Olgierd Wojtasiewicz. 1974, XV + 460 pp.

63. SÖREN STENLUND (ed.), *Logical Theory and Semantic Analysis. Essays Dedicated to Stig Kanger on His Fiftieth Birthday.* 1974, V + 217 pp.

64. KENNETH F. SCHAFFNER and ROBERT S. COHEN (eds.), *Proceedings of the 1972 Biennial Meeting, Philosophy of Science Association,* Boston Studies in the Philosophy of Science (ed. by Robert S. Cohen and Marx W. Wartofsky), Volume XX. 1974, IX + 444 pp. Also available as paperback.

65. HENRY E. KYBURG, JR., *The Logical Foundations of Statistical Inference.* 1974, IX + 421 pp.

66. MARJORIE GRENE, *The Understanding of Nature: Essays in the Philosophy of Biology,* Boston Studies in the Philosophy of Science (ed. by Robert S. Cohen and Marx W. Wartofsky), Volume XXIII. 1974, XII + 360 pp. Also available as paperback.

67. JAN M. BROEKMAN, *Structuralism: Moscow, Prague, Paris.* 1974, IX + 117 pp.

68. NORMAN GESCHWIND, *Selected Papers on Language and the Brain,* Boston Studies in the Philosophy of Science (ed. by Robert S. Cohen and Marx W. Wartofsky), Volume XVI. 1974, XII + 549 pp. Also available as paperback.

69. ROLAND FRAÏSSÉ. *Course of Mathematical Logic* – Volume II: *Model Theory.* 1974, XIX + 192 pp.

70. ANDRZEJ GRZEGORCZYK, *An Outline of Mathematical Logic. Fundamental Results and Notions Explained with all Details.* 1974, X + 596 pp.

75. JAAKKO HINTIKKA and UNTO REMES, *The Method of Analysis. Its Geometrical Origin and Its General Significance.* 1974, XVIII + 144 pp.

SYNTHESE HISTORICAL LIBRARY

Texts and Studies
in tye History of Logic and Philosophy

Editors:

N. KRETZMANN (Cornell University)
G. NUCHELMANS (University of Leyden)
L. M. DE RIJK (University of Leyden)